FRANCHISE VISION

Transform Your Future Through
Franchise Ownership

By
DAVID BUSKER

www.franchisevision.com

This book is dedicated to my father, who risked everything to start his own business and provide a better life for his family. His spirit of lifelong learning and deep caring for others inspires me to be my best self.

CONTENTS

INTRODUCTION

grew up in an entrepreneurial family. My dad started his own business at age 42. He did not have a college degree, and we had no money. He worked in a low paying farm machinery mechanic position for many years but had a deep-seated desire to do something on his own. He worked weekends custom harvesting for landowners and finally built up enough money to start his own business. I think I inherited his itch, although as an academic kid, I followed the traditional education and career track of many white-collar professionals. It was great until it wasn't.

After a pretty long tenure at a Big Six accounting firm, I spent five years with a Fortune 500 telecommunications firm where I was suddenly in the wrong seat one day when a new executive came in to head my department and brought his team from his former company. That was my first experience with the downside of being a corporate employee.

I next chose to move to a smaller regional company, where I could control my destiny better as a senior executive, joining as CFO and soon after being promoted to CEO. It was a good match with my skills, and I could build equity, which was the best of both worlds. Until the family that owned it put in place a new legal board of directors, who quickly decided that outsourcing the management of its real estate portfolio was the best decision. Now at the peak of my career, I was once again in need of a new direction. This was my trigger to take charge of my destiny and move to self-employment.

I had ignored the franchise consultants who chased me ever since my C-suite resume started floating around cyberspace. After a short stint with a startup company, however, I finally decided to sit down and listen after getting an email from a diligent consultant. After going through the process, my consultant did a great job adhering to my specific requirements and showed me a franchise that fit all my criteria.

I moved forward and started a franchise, a new boutique fitness concept, where I became the first location in Missouri and forged a new path to building a career that did not rely on an employer. I made the transition to self-employment by entering the world of franchising.

Being a franchise business owner has been a humbling yet empowering and deeply gratifying experience. While I've been tested in new, unanticipated ways, I've been rewarded many times over and created a lifestyle I've long sought. Today, I have control over my professional destiny. I work from home, set the schedule for involvement in my businesses, and enjoy prioritizing my family through a flexible lifestyle. I own a semi-absentee fitness franchise that generally requires five to ten hours per week. I spend most of my time helping others down the path of franchise ownership as a franchise consultant. As I grow more franchise locations, I can leverage my time even more.

So, as a long-time entrepreneur, small business CEO, franchisee, and now a franchise consultant, I wrote this book from a rich set of viewpoints. As a former CPA and CFO, analyzing risk and underwriting investments is second nature to me. As an entrepreneur creating new business models, I have learned that risk is mitigated through education, careful due diligence, and a willingness to do whatever it takes to succeed. As a franchisee, I have experienced the emotional arc required to move from employee to business owner, as well as the challenges and rewards of running one's own business. Finally, as a father of triplets, I have learned that happiness is in the journey, not the destination. I hope you find my insights useful in your exploration of business ownership.

Deciding to start your own franchise business is a discovery process that requires an intense and emotional journey over a short period. Candidates for franchise ownership often move from zero knowledge of franchising to beginning their life's most significant investment of time and money in about eight short weeks. This book is designed to mimic that journey chronologically and answer your most pressing gateway questions to learn if franchising is right for you and how to investigate a franchise.

After several years of working in franchising, I found a recurring need to educate my candidates and others about how to think about and investigate a franchise business. Franchised businesses take all forms—some are Fortune 500 companies, some are startups, and some are family-owned. Like any group of companies, some are good, and some are bad. The purpose of this book is to be a guide for you to investigate a franchise business and help you make a decision—yes or no—about whether a franchise brand is the right one for you.

After reading this book, you should:
- Understand the basics of franchise ownership
- Understand the typical process for investigating franchises
- Have a good idea if you are a candidate for franchise ownership
- Know how to start looking for the perfect franchise

What you will learn in this book:
- The steps to researching and buying a franchise
- Where to focus your efforts during your investigations
- Key things you will need in place to buy a franchise
- Red flags and cautions to consider before buying a franchise
- How to use advisors and consultants in your research process
- How to cope with the roadblocks and obstacles that may arise as you contemplate a franchise

I hope this book serves as a useful guide to exploring franchise ownership. I want to share with you my very best wishes for your success in achieving your vision.

Now go and discover franchising. Cheers!

THE EMOTIONAL
REQUIREMENT

> The beginning is the most
> important part of the work.
>
> P L A T O

There's likely a compelling reason you're reading this book. Something has shifted your thinking from your current situation, career or business to consider franchise ownership. Or maybe you're just curious about franchising. It's everywhere around us, yet a real mystery for many people.

Many people are curious about franchising. I speak with people every day to educate them about franchising and help them explore their potential as a franchisee. However, a much smaller number of people are motivated to change their lives for the better through action. It's often a journey of self-discovery to explore career alternatives, research business ownership, and ultimately decide to move forward in a new direction. Some people complete this process quickly. Others may have the itch but wait a year or two until they feel they are ready. It's unique to each person. In my experience, the catalyst to act, purchase a franchise, and start your own business requires two types of motivation.

MOTIVATION 1: THE TRIGGER

First, you need what we will call the trigger. A trigger is an event in your life that forces you to open your eyes, look around, and seek out change. This could be losing a job after a long career, the culmination of years of frustration with corporate America, or just a sudden urge to diversify as an existing business owner.

Whatever the reason, something prompts you to change your circumstances. We could also call this the negative motivator, although the meaning here is just that you are motivated to upend the status quo.

I've had displaced corporate executives, employed corporate executives, investors looking to diversify, current franchisees wanting to expand or diversify with a new brand, and many other types of people looking to transform their future. The one thing they all have in common is an urgent need to change the status quo, frustration with their current situation, or a feeling that they need to row their metaphorical boat in a new direction.

REAL WORLD EXAMPLE

Ken was a successful operations executive in a publicly-traded company that had gone through multiple acquisitions. After he was laid off, he realized he was worn out with the corporate bureaucracy and leadership vacuum. He longed to

*have his efforts be directly correlated with his outcomes. This
event was his trigger. He quickly grasped the franchise process
and embraced the investigation of multiple franchise brands.
After narrowing his choices, he chose a box lunch catering
and delivery franchise that allowed him to be full-time with
low overhead and scale the business quickly while creating the
opportunity to transition management to a manager and free up
his time to grow the business and pursue other opportunities.*

MOTIVATION 2: THE POSITIVE FUTURE VISION

Second, to move forward and act, you need a positive motivator.
This should take the form of a vision of a future state you would
like to realize. Can you visualize your future state?

For many years I have had a clear vision of my future. Instead
of traditional retirement, I envision owning multiple businesses,
real estate, and investments that are semi-absentee so I can both
control and make the most of my time, whether for work, family,
charity, or other pursuits. I'm a builder, so I like to spend time
building a business, let it get going, then begin building another
business while reaping the benefits of my previous efforts.

For me, I think my ultimate vision is one that is a combination
of entrepreneurial spirit and seeking autonomy. I've always wanted
to have the flexibility of time while building income streams and
businesses. And while I actively seek control of time, I don't expect
I will ever retire. Time is the new currency, and whoever controls
it, in my opinion, wins the game.

Your vision may be entirely different—spending more time
with family, traveling, or building a legacy for your children. As

long as you have a vision of your future, your highest achievement of goals and objectives, then you are on the right track to reaching them. You are always more likely to hit the target if you aim.

I have worked with hundreds of candidates, and there is a common theme I have learned about this. If someone doesn't know what they are trying to accomplish in the future or doesn't have a defined goal or aspiration, then they are not going to be a candidate for owning a business. It is great to dream about the future. But to realize it, you need to have a defined goal or destination you can visualize.

> ### REAL WORLD EXAMPLE
>
> Steve was a successful medical sales representative looking to exit corporate America soon. Like Ken, Steve was looking to control his destiny and see his efforts reflected in his outcomes. Steve achieved his goal by launching three units in an eyelash extension franchise, which allowed him to be semi-absentee while he kept his corporate position.

PUTTING IT TOGETHER: THE PATH FORWARD

So, think about your future. Can you visualize it? If you're only interested in a steady paycheck, being a weekend warrior, and never worrying about business after 5:00 p.m., then franchise ownership may not be right for you. There is no franchise where you can be purely passive, don't have to work, or can avoid all risks.

Once you have established your vision of the future, you must believe that franchise ownership can help you get there. If you believe franchising is a possible path to help you achieve the goals you have laid out, then it is likely you can seriously investigate a franchise business and move forward. In my experience, anyone who can't see the future picture of them owning a business and what outcomes that may bring to their life is not ready to take the next step. They may research brands and do a lot of tire-kicking, but won't ultimately decide to move forward.

Believing in the way forward doesn't have to happen right away, and you don't need some grand vision to achieve it. You simply need to believe a new path is a better alternative than your current path. To quote Robert Frost, do you choose to take the path less traveled? It can make all the difference.

If you find energy in a lifestyle of controlling your schedule, directing an organization, being part of the community, leading a team, constructing a sustainable business or string of companies, and building equity in a valuable enterprise, then franchising could be a perfect fit for you.

REAL WORLD EXAMPLE

Laura and Vince were a married couple with young kids and two corporate jobs. Vince worked for the government, and Laura was in sales. They had explored franchising by attending conferences and researched hundreds of brands. They were dead set on starting their own business. They had a positive future vision of what they wanted: flexibility, meaningful work, and a company that could scale while not sacrificing their family life. Once they were introduced to a brand that fit their criteria and future vision, they moved quickly to begin their new national nail care franchise.

SUMMARY

Starting a franchise business requires a serious emotional commitment. Aside from the facts, figures and due diligence of investigating a brand, moving forward requires three emotional changes:

- *The Trigger.* This is a compelling reason you want to change the status quo from your current career or business situation. This could be a job transition, frustration in your current career, or a desire to diversify.

- *Positive Future Vision.* This is a well-formulated vision of the future out at least five years, encompassing your daily work environment and the lifestyle you want to lead. The more specific your vision is, the more likely you will have the motivation to move forward.

- *Putting it Together.* While both a trigger and a positive future vision are necessary components to compel you to pursue business ownership, you must also believe that starting a franchise business can help you achieve your vision. Without that belief, you won't be able to bridge the gaps from due diligence to starting your journey.

02

ENTREPRENEUR OR EMPLOYEE: MINDSET

> Two roads diverged in a wood and I – I took the one
> less traveled by, and that has made all the difference.
>
> ROBERT FROST

As discussed in the previous chapter, there needs to be a motivational trigger for most people to contemplate business ownership. The bigger the trigger, the stronger the motivation to take action. For many of my candidates, this trigger can be losing a corporate position in middle management after many years or even decades working as part of corporate America. Suddenly being an employee doesn't feel so safe.

While some people feel compelled or find it necessary to leave the world of employment, others have the option to continue working as an employee. Finding any job as an employee may feel less risky by taking the more traveled road. The emotional battle between the perceived risk reduction of being an employee versus the benefits of business ownership is at the crux of the decision to start a business.

Not everyone has this emotional battle. For someone like Steve Jobs, it wasn't a drive for rewards versus safety that motivated him—it was simply how he was wired. These types of entrepreneurs see their path as less risky than giving up control of their careers to someone else. They are unemployable. They would be bored and frustrated if they had to work as an employee.

Candidates for franchising are different. They are entrepreneurial to consider franchising, but they aren't usually born that way. They are drawn to entrepreneurship for the rewards—financial, emotional, and aspirational—of controlling their destiny. And the rewards are many—there is no question your quality of life will increase as an entrepreneur. But they often have a choice of which road to take—employee or entrepreneur.

The transition from employee to entrepreneur and business owner requires a franchisee candidate to consider their mindset in different critical areas. These include their incentives for working, view of risk, desire for status, and whether they have a scarcity or abundance mindset.

INCENTIVES

As employees, particularly in larger corporate environments, we tend to develop certain habits. These habits can be hard to break in the transition to an entrepreneurial mindset. Most of the time, you aren't even aware of these habits.

Due to all the daily input we receive over many years, we slowly develop our innate, subconscious responses to stimuli, particularly in the business world. Changing that programming will be a requirement to start a business.

The difference in how they receive financial rewards is one of the most significant contrasts between an employee and an entrepreneur. An employee is paid for time. An entrepreneur is paid for results. This contrast in incentives is a vast difference between the mindset of an entrepreneur and an employee. Due to evolutionary forces, changing our mindset can take some effort.

An employee has an incentive to adopt a short-term mindset, such as focusing on finishing a project by the end of the day so they can hit the lake for the weekend. An entrepreneur has a more long-term mindset like an investor. They see every moment of how they spend their time as either moving toward their goal or away from it.

Incentives are a vast difference between employees and entrepreneurs. Consider your short and long-term goals. Aligning your short-term behaviors with your long-term goals is the key. It doesn't have to disrupt your lifestyle necessarily, but it may require adjustments. My family adjusted to me working Saturday mornings in my business—I bring my kids as additional help, so I get quality time and some extra hands. And I do back-office activities on Sunday morning while my teenage kids are still asleep. But I know my daily activities contribute to my long-term goal.

VIEW OF RISK

There have been many studies about the human bias for loss aversion. If the odds are precisely equal, people would much rather avoid losing $10 than having the possibility of winning $100. It does not make sense logically. But as with all biases, aversion to loss has roots in evolution. I assume our ancestors were much more motivated by avoiding the saber-toothed tiger than the reward of food that may be in the tiger's territory.

There have also been many studies of successful entrepreneurs. The great majority of them do not tend to be the wild-eyed visionaries that splash the covers of business magazines. They are diligent, hard-working people who take well-considered and educated risks to take control of their destinies. Many of them do that through franchising, which mitigates many of their concerns about starting a business.

An employee doesn't need to take any risk to get their paycheck every two weeks. Most corporate employees won't receive stock in the company or a big reward if they take a chance and succeed. But if they take a chance and fail, they will likely be reprimanded or could even lose their job. It's an unfortunate outcome of the corporate structure.

We would not have the iPhone, Amazon, or many of the transformative new businesses that have raised our quality of life without entrepreneurs overcoming every obstacle and assuming every risk to achieve their vision. The decision to start a franchise business is an entirely different and less transformative type of risk, but the emotional arc can have similar elements.

Steve Jobs never had to make a transition to be an entrepreneur—he didn't see obstacles as failures but rather stepping stones to his vision. He was hard-wired with a fearless mindset. You certainly don't need to be Steve Jobs to open a franchise business—that's the point! But you do need to address your view of risk directly when considering either staying an employee or becoming a business owner.

To produce results, the entrepreneur must take both financial and emotional risks. Losing money, losing time, or a failed venture are all possibilities. Most people will avoid these types of risks in return for the day-to-day safety of a paycheck, even if it comes with a soul-crushing existence. But those that can think differently about risk get disproportionately rewarded.

The legendary investor Warren Buffett is famous for several sayings regarding risk. One quote is, "Risk comes from not knowing what you're doing." This means you need to get informed and educate yourself. You can mitigate at least some risk by merely learning more about what you want to do. A second quote is, "We simply attempt to be fearful when others are greedy and to be greedy only when others are fearful." This ties directly to seeing opportunity when others may be scared—the best profits are made when purchasing at the bottom and the market is terrified. By changing your view, along with education and due diligence, you can take advantage of opportunities.

REAL WORLD EXAMPLE

In my fitness studio, it was terrifying at first to contemplate finding and retaining employees. However, by being diligent in every part of the hiring process, relying on my franchisor, using best practices of my fellow franchisees and having a mindset of continuous improvement, I have learned that for each employee that leaves, it is an opportunity to increase the quality of my team by adding someone better. I now have the confidence to overcome this and other obstacles by changing my mindset.

Like your body, exercising your risk muscle makes it stronger. Pretty soon, barriers that were previously terrifying seem miniscule. Asking for help from your bank, making payroll, or replacing your general manager may seem frightening at first. But once you start these daily activities of an entrepreneur, you gain confidence that suddenly turns seeing risks into seeing opportunities.

DESIRE FOR STATUS

Another evolutionary trait we all have is the need to be liked. It is subconscious, subtle, and no one is immune to it. Only truly transcendent achievers can let go of this and be their 100 percent authentic selves. We all need the approval of others at some level.

Entrepreneurs understand this part of human nature and take advantage of it. You can see this in social media, inflationary job titles, and the trend for self-promotion. Businesses may give away fancy job titles if it means they can pay less. This is playing on the human need for status.

Even entrepreneurs have this need. Who hasn't seen the CEO title of someone self-employed without any employees? I see it also every day. Aside from controlling their destiny, many franchise candidates in my experience want to build a prestigious business.

In contemplating franchise ownership, addressing this need for status objectively should be part of the process. If a franchise business provided exactly the lifestyle and income you want but is in residential cleaning or portable toilets, how would you feel about it? Many of the most successful franchises are in ubiquitous, everyday essential services that are not glamorous.

Consider your need for how you want to be perceived. True entrepreneurs aren't looking for public validation but rather internal validation. Being independent of your environment will remove this roadblock from your path.

SCARCITY VS. ABUNDANCE

As you can tell by now, emotional qualities need to be viewed through an evolutionary lens. The emotional requirement is the biggest hurdle you will face in your journey to become an entrepreneur. Going against your evolutionary emotional wiring may be necessary to achieve your goals.

Employees over time may naturally develop a scarcity mindset. The corporate structure leads you to believe you can't move up unless someone moves out. Or you come to think it's a zero-sum game in the business world. This can bring on a fatalistic viewpoint that leads employees to do the least amount necessary to get by since they don't feel any of their efforts will change anything. Or it can lead business owners to focus on pinching pennies and cause them to miss out on growing revenue.

Successful entrepreneurs, on the other hand, typically come from an abundance mindset. They know all the revenue, customers, and solutions are out there for the taking. Their challenge is only having enough time and balancing priorities to allocate resources to get the rewards. They know there will be obstacles, but they are confident they can focus extreme efforts on any problem and find a solution.

I have come to learn the real meaning of the "I don't have

time" or "I'm too busy" excuses we all make. What we are really saying is, "I can't prioritize this." We all have the same number of hours in the day, so why are some people successful in business and others not? Successful entrepreneurs avoid limiting beliefs and a scarcity mindset while prioritizing what matters to succeed.

GRIT AND CONTINUOUS IMPROVEMENT

A common trait of elite athletes takes our evolutionary viewpoint into account in a unique way. We know the avoidance of pain is a more significant motivator than the prospect of reward. But which kind of pain? For most of us, avoiding the effort required to be an elite athlete would be plenty of motivation to avoid that path.

However, it has been shown that a common trait among elite athletes—those at the very pinnacle of their sport—is that their drive comes not from the reward of winning, but their hatred of losing. They have the grit and drive to continuously improve and will do whatever it takes not to fail. Like an elite athlete, by doing whatever it takes to avoid failure in your business, you will likely raise your performance to the highest levels. You will be amazed at what you are capable of with the right mindset.

Much of what drives the entrepreneur mindset as compared to the employee mindset is never being satisfied. Entrepreneurs are always looking for continuous improvement—in themselves and their business. While they may accomplish this in many ways, you can harness this through education—learn as much as possible about how to achieve your goals.

As an example, you can currently get a Kindle Unlimited

membership from Amazon for $9.99 per month, allowing you access to thousands of non-fiction business books on every topic. That is affordable education for you to mitigate risk and study business strategies for every part of your small business. But it may require you to ditch some leisure activities that were otherwise filling your schedule.

To be an entrepreneur, you must be all-in emotionally and enjoy continuous improvement. If you are satisfied with the status quo and have a mindset of not fixing things that aren't broken, you should reconsider if starting a business is for you. Success in the business world requires constant adaptation but is a beautiful discovery process for the adventurous. And it is never dull.

THE ENTREPRENEURIAL MINDSET

Employees are paid for their time, and entrepreneurs are paid for their results. As a result, employees develop different mindsets than entrepreneurs. Due to our survival instincts, fear of failure, and how we developed through evolution as humans, the challenge for employees who desire to start a business is in the emotional transition to adopt an entrepreneurial mindset.

The entrepreneurial mindset can be achieved through a paradigm shift in your thinking, supported by education, research, letting go of your ego, and doing whatever it takes to make your dream realized. It doesn't have to be expensive, and you can balance your quality of life like any other challenge if you are committed.

If you believe you are stuck in an employee mindset and only see risk instead of opportunity, do more research, explore your why, and ask the deep questions. Get away from short-term thinking—focus on your long-term goals and then adapt your short-term behaviors accordingly. You have it in you to change your mindset and become an entrepreneur!

SUMMARY

Adopting the entrepreneurial mindset is a crucial step in your journey to business ownership. Evolution has wired humans to emotionally avoid risk, which folds exactly into the employee mindset. To overcome an employee mindset, we need to consider five areas and change our paradigm related to each:

- *Incentives.* Employees are paid for time, and entrepreneurs are paid for results. Changing our mindset to align our short-term behaviors with our long-term goals will free us from the trap of short-sighted employee thinking, even if it feels like there is risk reduction in that path.

- *View of Risk.* Risk and opportunity are two sides of the same coin. Changing your perspective from reacting to all stimuli as threats and instead asking yourself how your reaction can improve your position will turn risks into opportunities.

- *Desire for Status.* We all have a need for status with others; we are social animals. Fear of public failure and professional humiliation can be strong influences to avoid taking the step to start a business. Taking a careful inventory of who really matters to you and how important it is what others think can help you work through this.

- *Scarcity vs. Abundance.* Employees tend to have a scarcity mindset, while entrepreneurs tend to have an abundance mindset. There are multiple ways to win, and success is not a zero-sum game (or the economy would never grow).
- *Grit and Continuous Improvement.* Top athletes turn their hatred of losing into the determination to do whatever it takes to win and motivation to grind it out on a daily basis. If you don't have a mindset of continuous improvement, you may not be cut out to be an entrepreneur.
- *The Entrepreneurial Mindset.* Overcoming long-ingrained thought patterns from working in a corporate environment as an employee for many years is not easy. But with the right mindset, you can release yourself from these burdens and find a positive path forward that you may have never previously believed existed.

03

FRANCHISING AND TYPES OF FRANCHISES

> A person who never made a mistake
> never tried anything new.
>
> ALBERT EINSTEIN

So, what is a franchise? For most people, the word franchise evokes an image of the Golden Arches, the trademark of McDonald's. However, franchising is way more than fast food. Yes, restaurants are everyday businesses with hundreds of franchise brands, and yet, franchises exist in nearly every service industry. Any company that can benefit from proper branding, repeatable processes, and continuing product or service evolvement is a candidate to be franchised.

According to the International Franchise Association (IFA), franchising is a method for expanding a business and distributing goods and services through a licensing relationship. A franchisor is a company that grants a license to a franchisee for conducting business under its brand, trademarks, trade dress, policies, and procedures. The franchisor will specify the products and services to be offered by the franchisee and provide them with an operating system and support in addition to the brand. In exchange for the licensing, training, support, and other system benefits, a royalty is paid to the franchisor. While this royalty is nearly always a percentage of revenue, there are a few variations.

"Business opportunities" are another category of business licensing that doesn't rise to the level of a franchise. These usually involve a license but not a franchise agreement. Definitions can vary by state, but such an endeavor is generally defined as a packaged business investment that allows a buyer to begin a business. The Federal Trade Commission and 25 states currently regulate the concept. The thing to remember is that while all franchises are business opportunities, not all business opportunities are franchises.

Business opportunities will typically offer training, licensing, certification, and possibly equipment in exchange for a one-time license fee rather than ongoing franchise royalties. You have no control over the quality of others who purchase the same business opportunity or where they locate their company, and you have little or no support once you open the business. Therefore, you should exercise caution in exploring or considering business opportunities as investments.

FRANCHISE INDUSTRIES

As discussed earlier, franchising is not all about fast food. It's not even mostly about fast food. Service franchises are the name of the game in today's franchising space. Service franchises span a wide range but generally avoid the pitfalls and challenges of retail in the age of Amazon.com and trying to capture the modern trend, especially among younger generations, who value experience over material items. Most service-based franchises generally have lower startup costs and better margins than restaurants. Of course, everyone needs to eat, so the demand for this type of franchise is strong. Therefore, choosing a service franchise should be a careful exercise in making sure it has a lasting market and isn't a fad.

Restaurants aren't bad businesses. Indeed, there's a restaurant that started its first location in my neighborhood and became so successful it gained national attention and started franchising, all while making a healthy profit.

However, restaurants carry specific characteristics that make them more of a niche in the franchising world. Nearly all restaurant franchises require the owner to run the business day-to-day. They're best-suited to those who have restaurants in their blood and fully understand the hands-on nature of the industry. Many who consider franchise ownership want to own a prestigious business. This is understandable. You've worked hard for years. If you're going to enter the business world as an owner, you should be proud of your company. However, franchising isn't always super glamorous. Franchises often perform best in fragmented, ubiquitous industries where customer service, communication, technology, and other essential attributes of modern commerce are lacking.

Consider Great Clips, which started in 1982 and revolutionized the haircare industry by offering affordable, branded, walk-in hair services at convenient hours across the nation. Today, it continues to innovate with technology improvements and other enhancements that anyone owning an independent store would be challenged to replicate.

While hair care may not be overly glamorous, it provides steady, repeat business that can't be outsourced or sold on Amazon. com. You may think there are national brands in every industry, but there are many fragmented industries just now being revolutionized with trending franchise brands. As examples, the first national brands in nail salons and tree services have emerged recently.

THE FRANCHISE CONTINUUM

There are more than 3,000 registered franchise brands in the U.S., covering almost every industry. Some are family-owned, some are startups, and some are Fortune 500 companies. The types, sizes, and maturity of franchise companies are all over the board. However, in general, there are some consistencies.

Franchising is ideally suited to service franchises where there's a repeatable process, often recurring revenue and/or repeat customers. Active and growing franchising industries include health and wellness, beauty, fitness, residential services, commercial services, automotive, child enrichment, haircare, home healthcare, and many more. There's no real limit to the businesses that can have a franchise business model – I have even worked with a cremation franchise.

Franchise company business models run along what I describe as the Franchise Continuum, from low cost, self-employment options, all the way to multimillion-dollar investments like hotels. The most significant tradeoff as you span the continuum is investment level versus time involvement.

On the lowest investment end, there are opportunities we can call self-employment options as part of a larger group called *owner-operator* business models. Some in the industry may use the phrase "buying yourself a job," which can have a negative connotation, but there's nothing wrong with being self-employed and controlling your own destiny. In today's gig economy, there's an even larger movement toward independent contractors and self-employment.

Some attributes of what we call *owner-operator* franchises:

- Low investment level
- Few or no employees
- Full-time franchisee
- The franchisee is the primary driver of business – sales or customer service role
- Quicker ramp to cash flow
- Revenue more dependent on franchisee or sales activities
- Highest return on invested capital
- Lower return on invested time
- More difficult to scale due to the full-time franchisee role

On the higher investment end, some options are much higher-cost but require less time from the franchisee. The industry refers to these as *semi-absentee* or *manager-managed* models, requiring as little as 5 to 10 hours per week from the franchisee when stabilized. Some brands can even behave similarly to real estate, with a minimal owner time commitment.

Some attributes of semi-absentee franchises:

- High investment level
- Manager run with a team of employees or passive with no employees needed

- Part-time for franchisee
- Franchisee works on the business, not in the business
- Slower ramp to cash flow
- Durable, repeat revenue over time, more dependent on marketing activities
- Good return on invested capital
- Higher return on invested time
- Easier to scale multiple units or territories

There is a wide range of franchise business models, but you will find a general trade-off between investment levels and franchisee time involvement. Thus, higher cost, semi-absentee business models can have the owner fully involved or most allow the business to be manager-managed. The most critical criteria to set for your franchise business is franchisee involvement. Every brand will have a definition of the franchisee role.

YOUR PLACE ON THE FRANCHISE CONTINUUM

Before beginning your franchise search, you have to decide what role you will have in the business as a franchisee. Franchise brands are structured in how they define franchisee involvement. It's crucial to understand this aspect of your plan, or you'll waste your time exploring mismatched franchise opportunities

Here are three broad categories of franchise brands used to describe franchisee involvement:

- *Owner-operator.* This category includes both self-employment options as well as larger, slightly more scalable brands that still require the franchisee to operate the business. These tend to be lower investments that will ramp quickly but need the franchisee to be present full-time and manage the business. The service is often provided at the customer's location, so these are usually run from a home office and have very little overhead. These can be business-to-business ("B2B") or business-to-consumer ("B2C") brands.

REAL WORLD EXAMPLE

A great example of a self-employment option is Budget Blinds. Budget Blinds is a long-established, national brand that provides made-to-order blinds for consumers and businesses. This is a company with a low investment level that offers a path to business ownership for many younger professionals. You have no employees but work as the head of sales and customer service for your business, while the franchise company handles the calls and makes most of your appointments. Your role would be to meet with clients, close the sale, then order the blinds, and manage installations. You can control your schedule by managing your calendar availability.

REAL WORLD EXAMPLE

Mosquito Hunters is a mosquito-focused pest control company and an example of an owner-operator brand. While the owner doesn't conduct any direct pest control, he or she does need to run the business directly on a daily basis, oversee employees, and manage sales, marketing, and customer service. Because it builds a staff, this type of business can scale more quickly than a self-employment option to multiple territories by adding more trucks as the business grows.

- *Executive.* These are generally franchise brands that require a franchisee to be full-time to ramp up the business but can have managers running the staff to provide the product or service. These tend to be more scalable, and often the franchisee can back off in a few years after the business is established to have managers run the day-to-day. These business models tend to provide the product or service at the customer's location, reducing the need for and cost of customer-facing real estate. These businesses may be operated from a home office or may require a low-cost real estate space for operations or employees. These can be B2B or B2C brands.

REAL WORLD EXAMPLE

Fish Window Cleaning is the only national brand focused on commercial window cleaning. As an executive owner, you wouldn't be cleaning windows, but you would be handling sales directly for the first six to twelve months by offering free estimates to local businesses and overseeing operations and customer service. Upon getting established, you would hire a sales manager and even a general manager to entirely run the business as semi-absentee after you give a full-time effort the first two or three years to launch the business.

- *Semi-Absentee - Manager-Managed.* This is a large and growing category of franchise brands. With the impressive gains in technology, marketing automation, and customer service platforms, many service businesses can run with reduced involvement from the franchisee. While there is generally less reliance on sales and more on marketing, these businesses can be manager-run. These are more expensive investments that usually require customer-facing real estate for operations to provide the product or service in a fixed location. These businesses are often repeatable or membership-based revenue models that can create durable income streams over time. These tend to be B2C brands, although there are some B2B options.

REAL WORLD EXAMPLE

My franchise is a semi-absentee boutique fitness business called CycleBar. Group fitness is a perfect example of a manager-run type of business. Providing the service requires only one full-time employee, the General Manager, while the staff and instructors are all part-time. Everything is scheduled, so tasks can easily be delegated or handled by software. Sales and bookings are made online through the digital platform, which I can monitor via a mobile app, allowing me to control my time and involvement to around five to ten hours per week.

How you will be involved and where you will be on the Franchise Continuum is the most critical component to understand when considering a franchise. Will you be full-time, replacing a previous job? Are you keeping your corporate position and want to build a multiple-location franchise company on the side? Alternatively, are you looking for a more passive investment? These are all critical considerations to nail down before you begin looking at specific industries or franchise brands.

SUMMARY

There are over 3,000 franchise companies in the United States at any given time. Like other companies, some are good, and some are bad. Filtering through all of them can seem an impossible task. But by defining your criteria, you can quickly narrow down the field and only focus on companies and brands that exactly match the traits you want in a business, while avoiding what you don't want.

- *The Franchise Continuum.* This is a reference to the trade-off of investment level and time commitment that is generally found in most franchise business models. Low investment business models tend to provide their service out in the community, or the franchisee can work from home, keeping costs low while they require a full-time commitment. High investment models tend to be manager-managed and may ramp more slowly but create repeat cash flow over time with less time involvement from the owner.

- *Owner-Operator.* On the lower end, owner-operator brands require the full-time commitment from the franchisee but typically have a lower capital investment.

- *Executive.* In the middle, these brands may require more time to get the business launched but may become manager-managed and be more scalable over time.

- *Semi-Absentee or Manager-Managed.* These brands allow the owners to keep a full-time job elsewhere and hire a manager to run the business. These require a higher capital investment but are more scalable and require less time commitment from the owner.

FRANCHISE COST AND RETURN ON INVESTMENT

> The secret to happiness is freedom...
> And the secret to freedom is courage.
>
> THUCYDIDES

One of the first questions I get from candidates is about franchise cost and how much they will make annually. While this is a question begging to be asked, it is not always easy to answer with a superficial response.

For a sense of scope, you should be able to easily find quoted ranges from the Franchise Disclosure Document, Item 7. This will show a low and high range, by line item, for your estimated initial cost in the franchise. While it is not a guarantee of what your costs will be, using it as a starting point and being conservative in your projections is the recommended path.

FRANCHISE COST

So, how much does a franchise cost? As discussed in the previous chapter, the answer covers a considerable range. The most significant factor in franchise cost is whether or not you will have customer-facing real estate.

On the lowest end, self-employment franchises may allow you to get started with as little as $50,000. For the cost of the franchise fee, computer equipment, marketing collateral, and software, you can get started. On the other end of the scale, a newly built hotel may cost $10 million or more to get open and operating.

A large majority of service franchise brands fall into a few categories. Note that every franchise outlines its respective estimated costs in Item 7 of the Franchise Disclosure Document, which is discussed in a later chapter, and that the amounts here are simply broad guidelines:

- Owner-Operator: $50,000 - $250,000 per unit or territory
- Executive: $100,000 - $350,000 per unit or territory
- Semi-Absentee or Manager-Managed: $250,000 - $2.5 million per unit or territory

Even within the same brand, one location may cost twice as much as another, depending on things like market conditions, labor union prevalence, the franchise owner's choice of real estate, and ability to negotiate a lease.

For purposes of this book, we will exclude discussion of franchises requiring standalone real estate, such as fast food or sit-down restaurants and hotels. These franchises likely require raising investor capital and generally require investments over $1 million for a single unit or territory. While this is a significant area of franchising, we will focus this discussion on franchises that can typically be started by an individual entrepreneur without raising investor capital.

FRANCHISE RETURN ON INVESTMENT – TIME, MONEY AND TALENT

Many who investigate franchises have difficulty projecting a rate of return on investment ("ROI") for a given franchise. They find there is variability not only among different brands but also within a single franchise brand. It can sometimes appear there is very little correlation between the total investment and the amount of money one can make in the business.

Every system has a franchisee that's at the top reaping financial rewards, and a franchisee who is dead last and could be either financially mediocre, or worse, desperate to get out of the system. So, while there is no rule of thumb that applies to ROI in franchise opportunities, understanding your investment is an excellent place to start.

The real answer may not be intuitive for most people. When you think of investing in real estate, the stock market, or other passive investments, there's a direct relationship between the amount invested and the total return. Returns of 10 to 15 percent per year on invested capital are typically considered very good, whether through dividends, interest, or capital gains. But these are passive investments. You are not spending much if any, time or expertise managing your investment on a daily basis.

The idea that the more you invest, the more you'll get back

doesn't necessarily apply to franchising. The investment is usually not passive, so that logic doesn't apply in the same fashion. In addition to your capital, you are investing a fair amount of your time and management skills as well. You should be able to achieve a good return on all three investments. Therefore, since you are making three investments, when you look at ROI in franchising, it should be considerably higher than what you can earn in a passive vehicle.

If the return isn't higher than what you could achieve in the stock market or real estate, what are you working for? You'd be better off keeping a corporate job and investing your capital passively. Another calculation is to compare your current or recent salary to the projected average cash flow from the franchise upon stabilization. Let's say you were making $100,000 per year in your previous job but now need to work full-time in the new business to only make $50,000. Even if the franchise results in a 100 percent return on invested *capital*, you won't feel it's a good investment of your time and skills.

Conversely, if you invest $100,000 of cash in a new franchise and finance the rest, where it produces $20,000 annually net but requires only one or two hours per week, you might say that's an excellent investment at a 20 percent return on capital because it requires hardly any of your time.

Let's explore some candidate profiles based on similar characteristics of many former candidates with whom I have worked.

Jake: Little Capital, Seeking Career Change

Jake is a hard-working sales guy who has experience in several industries. He has complete confidence in his skills and loads of determination, but has gone through a divorce and doesn't have a considerable nest egg. He wants a business that can provide significant income potential and scale to possibly a big company while having lower startup costs.

Jake requires a higher return on capital of 50 to 100 percent to get his income ramped up quickly. Jake has chosen to invest in a senior care franchise, which requires low start-up capital, but with full-time effort can scale rapidly to a million-dollar business with good margins.

Lisa: Lots of Capital, Seeking Transition

Lisa is a sales executive with a Fortune 500 company. She has been working in corporate America for 25 years, has significant retirement savings and sound investments, but she's looking to exit the employee world in the next few years. Since she is keeping her corporate position and still has kids in school, Lisa has limited time to start a new business. However, she has flexibility in her sales position to get things launched and eventually wants to run the business full-time once she can replace her current income.

Lisa chose to invest in a multi-unit beauty franchise where she can be semi-absentee while approaching 30 to 40 percent return on capital once established and create enough income to replace her current salary and leave corporate America to run her franchise full-time in a few years.

Rob: Lots of Capital, Investment Focus

Rob is a business owner already. He has multiple investments in companies and real estate and wants to diversify into franchising. Unfortunately, Rob doesn't have much time, and he has no interest in running a business with employees. Still, he's willing to work to get a *new passive investment set up if it will return better than real estate or stocks and bonds.*

Rob would be happy with a 15 to 20 percent return on capital if he doesn't have much time involvement. Rob chose a salon suites franchise, which behaves more like real estate, requires no employees, and is a perfect complement to his other business investments.

So, how do you find a franchise with high returns? As big things often come in small packages, the costliest franchise investment isn't always the first place to look. You may want to consider concepts with significant management leverage or semi-absentee business models. These can often be franchises with total investments of less than $250,000, and in some cases, less than $75,000 if you want to be full-time self-employed or owner-operator.

The next step is to carefully investigate the average earnings of a typical unit during the first three years of operation. Make sure you know the average performance, not just what the best units can achieve. Sensitize your projection by creating a baseline on the averages, then consider your best- and worst-case scenarios when projecting future financial performance.

Most franchises will provide financial averages in the FDD. If not, you will need to get this information through the validation process, which is covered in a later chapter. If the business does not project to perform and make the necessary returns by the third year, you should keep looking. There are plenty of great opportunities out there that will meet or exceed this standard in a relatively short time frame.

Don't be afraid to thoroughly vet multiple franchise business models to find the best combination of return on your time, expertise, and capital invested to reach your goals and objectives. The best source is always to validate any claims by the franchisor with actual franchisees in the respective systems.

SUMMARY

Franchise cost and return on investment are the first and most asked about topics when considering a franchise. What makes these questions so difficult to answer are the variables that go into each unit or location. Every franchise system will have a location that is number one and a location that is dead last in performance. And the most significant factors in success are the skills and determination of the franchise owner. So asking anyone, "how much money will I make?" is a loaded question.

- *Franchise Cost.* This will vary wildly depending on the brand, franchisee role, and whether it requires customer-facing real estate. Even within the same brand, there are huge swings in cost based on a multitude of factors.
- *Owner-Operator.* These business models vary but tend to range from $50,000 to $250,000 per unit or territory.
- *Executive.* These business models vary but tend to range from $100,000 to $350,000 per unit or territory.
- *Semi-Absentee or Manager-Managed.* These business models vary the most because they typically require customer-facing real estate. Even within a brand, the costs can vary wildly and require good local market due

diligence. The investment tends to range from $250,000 to $2.5 million per unit or territory.

Franchise return on investment is not as easy to calculate as a stock or bond. You are investing not only money but also time and expertise in your new business. And the rewards you get are not just financial. While the economic calculation must make sense and compare favorably to your other options, when calculating the return, don't forget about your time and expertise invested along with capital. Your quality of life is an essential factor in this calculation.

BEFORE YOU BEGIN:
BUILD A ROADMAP

*Patience, persistence, and perspiration make
an unbeatable combination for success.*

NAPOLEON HILL

Due to regulatory disclosure and timing requirements, the process of investigating a franchise and becoming a franchisee follows a similar process for all franchise brands. It's not always intuitive, and at certain times may seem a little rigid or frustrating, but understand that the process consists of a fair investigation process conforming to regulatory requirements that are designed for volume since the majority of candidates don't end up signing a franchise agreement.

Here are some things to expect from the process of becoming a franchisee:

- A six- to eight-week process on average but customized to your timeline
- Each brand will have a franchise development associate

assigned to you throughout your process

- It will take a commitment of time and engagement from you
- It needs to be a mutual fit – the brand is interviewing you to award a franchise at the same time you are evaluating the brand

Over the next two chapters, we will cover the steps or decisions you should expect to follow when you decide to investigate franchise ownership.

HIRE A CONSULTANT OR GO IT ALONE?

Before entering the franchise world, I wasn't aware that franchise consultants existed. In retrospect, it makes perfect sense due to the unusual nature of the franchise process, regulations, and the thousands of brands to sort through. I eventually learned all the various intricacies of the franchising process by going through it myself, including the emotional demands and challenges of changing my career, my industry, and executing a sizeable financial investment all at once. Now I help people every day to get through this same demanding process.

Imagine you move to a new city and need to find a new home. You're busy, you have a family, a job, and don't know the neighborhoods. You can undoubtedly look at homes online and buy a home yourself, but you will likely hire a professional real estate agent who knows the market and knows the local regulations. He or she can guide you through the process, assist you with setting your search criteria and use his or her access to listing services to help you find a home that you otherwise could not have found on your own.

While the actual contract to purchase a home is between you and the seller (you need to do your own home inspection), your real estate agent works on your behalf and can be invaluable. This scenario is a near-perfect analogy to a franchise consultant, although there is much more consulting involved in starting a franchise business than buying a home.

Like a real estate agent, franchise consultants are paid by the seller or franchisor. But they should not be sales agents for any brand. In fact, due to regulatory structures, consultants should specifically take a neutral stance among brands while still providing you all the resources and information to decide. Your real estate agent only wants you to find the right house and will seek to do an excellent job, so you refer them in the future. A good franchise consultant works the same way. They will want you to find the franchise that best fits you and develop a long-term relationship.

Another consideration in whether to hire a consultant is the relationship of the consultant and their network to the franchise brands. It's often the case that brands prioritize candidates from the top consulting networks and experienced individual consultants in those networks since the franchisor will know their candidates have been qualified, prepared, and well-matched to the brand before the first phone call. Franchisors have a much higher success rate with these types of candidates, and it allows them to be efficient with their time. They may not always prioritize candidates without a consultant or people who just request info on the website.

A good consultant works with these companies daily and knows precisely which brands have quality management teams, stable ownership, and great support for franchisees. They will also be the first to know when new brands launch, which can give you an edge if you are an early adopter or pioneer looking to get in early on a growing category.

Finally, franchise consultants are not all equal. Think of them like any other professional service provider, such as an attorney, real estate broker, or accountant. You need to find a practitioner with whom you can identify and who understands your needs and will be patient and work hard to help you achieve your vision.

Unlike some other professions listed, however, franchise consultants are not required to be licensed or complete continuing education, although there are industry certifications available with the International Franchise Association. Franchise consultants must be registered with the Federal Trade Commission and the handful of states that require it, but there are no continuing education requirements or licenses needed to become a consultant. Therefore, it creates a lower barrier of entry to do this type of work and makes it essential to find a quality consultant.

You should research a consultant's background, business experience, franchise experience, websites, LinkedIn profile, and publications as well as former candidate referrals to make an informed decision. Consultants may also be or have been franchisees, which can give them a valuable perspective, as they have walked your path.

In the end, you may decide you have enough business experience and wisdom to go it alone. If you have been a business owner previously, are comfortable making financial projections, and understand how to run a small business, you may be fine. But since consultants are paid on contingency by the franchisor and cost you nothing, you may decide your time is valuable, and having assistance will make your process more efficient.

If you're unsure whether to engage a consultant, you may want to consider interviewing several franchise consultants provided through trusted referral sources. Having an accomplished business professional who has many years of business leadership and franchise experience guide you through the process may provide benefits you should consider at no financial risk to you.

SETTING YOUR CRITERIA

Before considering industries or brands, it's critical to establish your criteria. The most important criteria you must determine is franchisee involvement (owner-operator, executive, or semi-absentee). This is an absolute requirement for you to match to the correct franchise, and there will be legal requirements in the franchise agreement addressing this directly.

If you have engaged a consultant, they will interview you in-depth to develop your criteria and understand your goals, objectives, and passions to best match you with brands that fit your franchisee profile. If you are working directly with franchisors, have the most critical components of your criteria ready for discussion to quickly eliminate brands you don't qualify for or don't match your criteria.

Consider your investment level, and if you must stretch financially to own a brand. You will want to be conservative and only enter a franchise agreement if you have the time, resolve, financial wherewithal, and financing to see it through break-even while covering your living expenses. All franchise brands will screen candidates financially by two criteria:

1. **Liquidity.** The franchisors want to see you have enough liquid capital to sign a franchise agreement (or development agreement for multiple units) and a source of funds or income to cover your living expenses while starting up.

2. **Net Worth.** The franchisors also want to make sure you have the balance sheet to finance the rest of your total investment and working capital beyond just your cash down payment.

Deciding on your investment level limit is obviously a crucial factor in your criteria. There are many considerations that can affect this decision, including how you finance your franchise investment. Financing your franchise will be discussed more in a later chapter.

Other criteria you need to consider before you engage with franchise brands:

- *Motivations.* Why are you looking now? Is it enough just to be frustrated in your current position or displaced? As discussed earlier, you need to have a positive future vision and believe that franchising can help you achieve it.

- *Business History.* Do you have enough experience to be comfortable running a business? You will have to make decisions in every area of business, including sales, marketing, operations, hiring, human resources, accounting, finance, and legal. Of course, you will hire third parties or use software tools to assist, but you need to be comfortable allocating resources, whether internal or external, to achieve your goals.

- *Geography.* Do you know where you want your business located? All franchises will have different requirements for territory. Some require you to live near your business, and some may even allow you to live in a different state.
- *Employees.* Are you okay leading a large group of employees? What about blue-collar or unskilled, higher turnover hourly positions? Consider your disposition on leading a team, going it alone, or having a small group of employees.
- *Hours and Workdays.* Are you strictly a nine-to-five type of person, or do you like to work flexibly? There are franchises for either. For instance, B2B franchises are typically only open Monday through Friday during regular business hours, which can be appealing to some people.
- *Risk and Security.* Are you a pioneer? Does the thought of an exciting new brand in an emerging category energize you? Or are you risk-averse and looking to only consider a brand with 100 or more locations and no closures? There are tradeoffs in that more established brands may have more limited territory available, while emerging brands may be in a fast-growth category and provide your choice of locations in your market.
- *Status.* This may sound unusual, but it's something to consider honestly. Many entrepreneurs need to find a passion or purpose in their business, and less glamorous routine services such as residential cleaning, while great financially, may not be in an industry that fits their social or personal identity. Are you passionate about owning a business, or only about owning a particular business?

- *Spouse.* You may be an entrepreneur at heart, but does
  your spouse share that vision? There may be different views
  of risk and business ownership. Getting a consensus with
  your spouse or partner early on in your process is critical
  to a successful outcome.

There are undoubtedly many other criteria you may consider
or have in mind. Make a list of the most important qualities to you,
follow your instincts and focus only on those franchise brands that
fulfill your needs

THE PASSION TRAP IN FRANCHISE SELECTION

After a career of working for someone else, many people want
to have more purpose in their daily work. Choosing something
you're passionate about as a business can be a great motivator. For
instance, many fitness enthusiasts find starting a fitness business is
an excellent marriage of their personal and professional interests.

However, in my experience, you should exercise caution here.
There are plenty of examples where people try to make their hobby
their business, only to end up hating their hobby and discovering
they went into the business for the wrong reasons. Obviously, you
need to believe in your product or service to be successful, but
it's most important to be passionate about owning a business in
general, versus focusing on a particular service or product. This
will help you be successful regardless of the industry or service
since your focus is on the organization rather than the widget.

Consider a former franchisee candidate we will call Jim. Jim was in sales and played golf whenever he could before he was downsized and decided to start a franchise. Because of his love of golf, he chose to open a golf store. Awesome, right? Well, Jim found out that a golf store wasn't really about enjoying golf but a retail and inventory-intensive business whose peak hours were on the weekend when he wanted to be on the golf course.

Jim hated his golf store business and decided to sell. If Jim had carefully thought about his business criteria instead of his hobby passion, he might have learned that a B2B franchise would have allowed him to focus on his skillset (sales), play golf in his business courting new customers, and give him freedom on the weekends to play golf since he was only selling to businesses during the week.

Carefully think through your criteria regardless of the product or service before you consider specific industries or brands to avoid the passion trap.

SUMMARY

Building a plan for your franchise investigation is a crucial step to set your frame of mind as you consider franchise ownership. I have seen too many people focus on a franchise brand from a consumer standpoint, only to get frustrated and disappointed after discovering they did not qualify, or it was not a fit for their goals.

There are several steps you can take at the beginning to make your franchise investigation productive and less frustrating while managing your expectations:

- *Hire a Consultant or Go It Alone.* You should consider whether hiring a consultant is valuable for you. Because a consultant works with franchise brands every day and costs you nothing, most candidates find it worthwhile to work with a quality consultant. But not all consultants are equal in skills and experience. Since it is not a licensed profession, rely on trusted referrals, or complete background research to find a quality consultant.

- *Setting Your Criteria.* Diving deeply into your requirements for a business while minimizing the consideration of industry is an essential activity before looking at specific brands. Among the most critical criteria is franchisee involvement in the business.

- *The Passion Trap.* Don't make your hobby your business. If you are already in an industry about which you're passionate, it can be positive to consider a franchise in that industry, such as a fitness professional becoming a fitness franchisee. However, you should generally exercise caution and focus on your business goals—you may find that your perfect business is in an industry you did not even consider.

THE FRANCHISOR
DISCOVERY PROCESS

Discovery consists of seeing what everybody
has seen and thinking what nobody has thought.

ALBERT SZENT-GYORGYI

f you are working with a consultant, they will use your criteria
to match you to brands that fit your model. If you are working
alone, you need to get the attention of the franchisor by
contacting them through their website or other channels. Once
you register with a franchise brand, it will qualify you and move
you into the discovery process.

The discovery process typically consists of a series of calls with
a franchise development representative that will last, on average, six
to eight weeks. These calls may vary by brand, but you should expect
similarities. In these calls you may discuss any or all of the following:

- Overview of the brand
- Videos/background information
- Unit economics

- Marketing
- Operations
- Training
- Franchise Disclosure Document (FDD)
- Validation with existing franchisees
- Discovery Day

THE FRANCHISE DEVELOPMENT TEAM

Imagine you need a midsize family sedan. You want a quality, durable, and affordable car for your family, so you narrow the choices to a Honda Accord or Toyota Camry. You go out on a Saturday and visit each dealership nearest you to see their inventory and get more information on the respective models. You may be leaning one way, but generally, know that either car is built by a company known for quality.

As you enter the first dealership, you can't find anyone to help you. Then you finally find a salesperson who is pushy or wants to get you into the chair in his or her office to begin negotiating before answering all your questions. Or you feel they are evasive. Regardless of how good that car brand is, you likely won't buy a car from that dealership.

Then imagine you go to the second dealership and have an excellent sales experience. You get all the information you need in a direct and honest way and feel no pressure. You've had a great experience with the dealership and will likely purchase from them, regardless of the product or brand.

I like to make this analogy to franchise candidates in describing the franchise development or sales process. Even if the franchise brand is a perfect fit, a terrible sales process will likely steer you away. Inadequate representation reflects poorly on a brand. I would like to say this never happens, but sometimes it does. By and large, the franchise developers I work with are supreme professionals, and I have developed solid relationships with them. However, the process does vary. Your best strategy is to make a good impression and form a strong bond with the franchise developer in the same way you would during an executive interview.

The franchise developer will run a structured process while providing you standardized information on the brand. They are typically paid on partial or full commission, so they have an incentive to sign new franchisees since the vast majority of franchise candidates fall out of the process. However, none of the quality franchise developers I work with have an interest in hurting their brand by recruiting unqualified franchise candidates. They also don't have the final say in whether you are awarded a franchise, so they want to find franchisees who are the right fit for their brand and will get approved by management.

Some franchise developers are relatively new, and some are industry veterans who have been doing this for many years. In either case, you should expect professionalism, honesty, and integrity in the franchise development process.

DISCOVERY DAY

Once you've established good rapport and mutual interest with a brand, have reviewed the FDD, and are in validation, the franchise development representative will likely invite you to Discovery Day, sometimes called Meet the Team Day. This is usually a one- or two-day event at the company's headquarters where you will get to know the founders and/or executive team, experience the brand or service firsthand, and meet the heads of operations, training, marketing, etc. as well as other franchise candidates.

Discovery Day is not a tire-kicking exercise. If you agree to attend Discovery Day, you should have decided already that this is your brand and completed all due diligence. Your goal for this event should be to absorb the company culture, look for any red flags, and decide from an emotional standpoint if these are people you can partner with. Despite all the formalities of the franchising process, these are real people running real companies and should be treated with the respect you would seek if you owned a company, so be professional and courteous while building relationships during your visit.

If you feel you are being sold to, it's sometimes easy to be skeptical. A good franchise investigation process should not make you feel that way. Indeed, every company wants to present themselves in a positive light, but they also don't want to award franchises to people who end up failing or have false expectations. Coming out of Discovery Day, you should feel a balance of appreciation for both the effort required and a real sense of positive future potential.

Here are several considerations to help you navigate your Discovery Day experience:

Prepare

If you have specific goals for Discovery Day, it is OK to let the franchisor know what you want to get out of your discovery day visit. Send them your list of questions prior to your arrival. This gives them a chance to prepare to address your specific issues or have personnel available if you have essential topics that only particular experts can answer, such as operations, marketing, etc.

Relax

By now, you should have completed the analytical part of your due diligence and made all necessary validation calls and financial projections. Take a breath and relax as you travel to Discovery Day. This part of the process is for you to sit back and absorb the brand, culture, and community of fellow franchisees. Take part in any networking or dinner events before the meetings and use the opportunity to get to know as many people associated with the brand as you can on a personal level.

Confirm Fit

Ask them why they think you are a good candidate for their franchise. This is a great topic to discuss in person.

Succession

Question the franchisor about their leadership succession plan. This is especially important if it is a young franchise company led by the founder.

- What if the founder/owner/company leader were to leave suddenly?
- Who is poised to take over company leadership if in this sort of situation? This is another good topic to discuss in person.

Be Candid But Professional

Don't feel you need to hold back—put forth any question or concern you have. Starting a franchise business is an important decision, and you need all facts to make a well-informed choice. But be respectful and professional—if you treat the franchisor as if you are negotiating for a car purchase, they may see that as a sign you are uncooperative or may not be a positive contributor or cannot follow a process.

- The best analogy is to treat it like a job interview, except without the serious interview questions.
- Follow the dress code for all events (if you don't know, ask your franchise developer), and use proper business etiquette.
- While it should be informative and will include social events, these events are for networking and getting to know the company and candidates. As with any company event or business conference, don't overdo it with cocktails and keep social and political opinions in check.

Be Strategic

If you attend a dinner event that is open seating, for example, be strategic in where you sit. Think about which person you may want to build a relationship with. You may only get occasional chances to get face-to-face time with the CEO, for example, so consider spending time with the founders or senior management on a personal level, so they know you in the future. You only have a short window of time to get to see the character of the brand, so think about how you can best experience the people and culture in the context of the trip agenda.

Be Engaged, But Not Aggressive

The brands will expect you to be engaged in the process, ask questions in meetings, and be outgoing. Similar to a prospective employer, they are looking for high-quality franchisees who can be successful in their system.

You should be finished with your due diligence prior to Discovery Day. If you are getting into the weeds or asking detailed questions that have already been answered, it may send the wrong signal to the franchisor. Ask high-level, insightful queries but don't plan for an inquisition.

Look for Cultural Fit

Similar to a job interview where you know the job description is perfect for you, but you want to understand the company, you will also want to absorb the culture of the company to determine if it is for you.

Alignment

Do you agree with the vision of the founders and their goals? Are these the kind of people you can partner with? Listen carefully to the words and watch the actions of the founders and executive team to determine if they have formed the company in a way you agree with. As you interact with the company leaders and folks who will train and support you, ask yourself:

- Do I like these people?
- Do I see myself enjoying working with these folks?
- Do I feel like I will fit into this club?
- Are we on the same page about how to operate and grow this company?

Mutual Fit

Remember, they are sizing you up just as you are sizing them up. Being prepared and putting your best foot forward is essential. Consider this just like a job interview—your primary goal is to get awarded a franchise. You can always decline the offer, but don't sabotage your chances by being too aggressive at Discovery Day.

Inside Information

Franchisors will share detailed and proprietary business practices at Discovery Day. They will likely show you more detailed information about their marketing systems, POS systems, operating procedures, etc.

Understand there is a limit as to what the franchisor will share. Some information will only be shared once you have signed a franchise agreement due to trademark and confidentiality reasons to protect their brand.

Decisiveness

Decisiveness is one of the essential qualities that define successful business owners. Attending Discovery Day is usually one of the later stages of the due diligence process; the finish line is in sight, and coming to a yes or no decision is imminent.

Expect the franchisor to ask you to commit to a decision date. They are looking for people who are excited about their business, believe they can be successful, confident in themselves, and are comfortable making decisions.

If you waver or cannot commit to a decision time frame, it may be a red flag to the franchisor; it suggests that the candidate is either not excited about the business or is either not confident in their ability to be successful or make decisions.

Be Ready for Yes or No

Communicate with the franchisor within 48 hours of concluding your Discovery Day visit. Let them know where you are in your decision process.

The Discovery Day can stimulate additional questions or points to be clarified—it is OK to request that information but resolve these questions quickly and get an answer to the franchisor.

Explore Your Emotions

As you travel back home from Discovery Day, notice what you are feeling and thinking.

- Are you feeling a sense of excitement?
- Do you find yourself visualizing yourself already running the business?
- Do you find yourself creating a mental list of all the details you need to take care of to get the business going?

If you answer yes to all these questions, this is your gut, letting you know that this business could work for you.

Understand Fear

A sense of excitement, if present, is also likely to be mixed with some feelings of fear. Remember that this is perfectly normal; you are taking a new direction in life, which is exciting but not familiar. Use fearful feelings to drive you to do as much due diligence as possible, but don't let these fears paralyze you or steal your dream—remember why you started this process.

You will never get to 100% confident of future success—

you only need to be 100% satisfied in your commitment to be successful. I always coach candidates that you can get to 95% confidence through due diligence and education, but you must bridge the last five percent through confidence in yourself that you can handle potential obstacles and unknowns.

Model out the worst-case scenarios and possible solutions or remedies to help manage emotions. Resolve that you will do whatever it takes to avoid failure, and it can be a massive boost to your mindset.

Franchise Signing

Some brands make the last part of Discovery Day a signing day, although this is not common. Ask about this ahead of time, so you understand the expectation.

Post-Discovery Day

Expect to make a verbal commitment within a few days after Discovery Day. Your franchise developer from the brand will call you to get a verbal YES or NO. Brands have been holding territory for weeks for you to get to this point and expect you to have your due diligence completed. Be prepared to say YES or NO quickly after your trip.

Franchise Agreement

If your decision is a YES, then they will send you signing documents and work on signing the franchise agreement shortly after your verbal confirmation. If you need an attorney to review the deal, they will give you a reasonable amount of time to do that.

Congratulations, you made it through Discovery Day! If you

have completed your due diligence and have been fully engaged, professional and positive with the franchisor throughout your process, it is very likely they will call you shortly after Discovery Day and award you a franchise.

The Management Team

Because franchise companies are all different, you may experience a wide range of structures regarding how they are managed and the level of people in decision-making roles. Some franchise companies are Fortune 500 type companies, while others may be startups or family-owned.

If you are energized by a family feel, would like to be involved in building a brand, and have the CEO on speed-dial, a startup or emerging brand may be a good fit for you.

On the other hand, if you like a large organization, black and white directions, support structures, and processes, then a well-established franchise with thousands of locations may be more suitable. Or something in between.

At Discovery Day, you should generally meet the senior management team, and if it's an emerging brand, the founders. This can be very valuable to understand the vision for the brand and to determine if you agree with where the brand is headed.

At a minimum, you should be able to meet with the management, operations, marketing, and other franchise support personnel that you would be working with as a franchisee. Gauge your confidence in the team and look for consistent quality and culture in the brand's management. Determine if these are people with whom you can partner and build relationships.

Franchisor Vision

It is worthwhile to try and investigate a franchise brand's organizational goals. Like any other company, they can be different. Some brands want to grow organically for the long term, and others desire to eventually sell the company to a private equity firm or strategic buyer. Or they may already be owned by a private equity firm so you can expect it to be sold in the next five years.

Note that even if a franchise company has an exit strategy in mind, that is not necessarily a bad thing. Sometimes a brand overgrows beyond the capabilities of the original franchisor, so being acquired by a much more established operator in that industry can be a good thing. I have seen this play out multiple times, so don't be scared off if a brand has ambitious plans for growth or exit strategies. In general, it can be a positive development depending on the brand.

Alternatively, I have worked with excellent, family-owned franchise brands that will not sell and desire only to grow slowly and steadily. This can be an attractive situation also. Ask questions and listen carefully to the senior leadership for guidance on what their future vision is for the company.

Considering the future vision or exit strategies of a franchisor need not be a decisive factor in your choice of a franchise brand, but it can help you better understand the goals and ambitions of the company to determine if they are in alignment with your goals. These things can often change with management, and ultimately, you won't have control over the future direction, but your franchise agreement guarantees your ability to own and run your business for the duration of the term.

Decision Time

Once you get home from Discovery Day, expect a phone call from your development representative asking if you are *in* or *out*. Most brands do not make Discovery Day a signing day, but they will want to know within a few days if you are planning on moving forward since they have been holding territory for you throughout the process. Territory is something that's first come, first served. So, if you are out, they will simply move on to the next candidate.

If you're not ready to move forward, stop your process and reevaluate. Is it because of the brand? Or would you have ended up rejecting any brand at this stage? Look deeply at why you started this process. Was it because you had a change in your career, and you were just curious, or do you have a vision of your future owning your own business? If you can't envision yourself running a business and the rewards just don't sync up with your perceived risks, then you may have learned that franchising is not for you.

If you emotionally cannot move to sign a franchise agreement, you may have learned you set the wrong criteria. Perhaps you're energized by the thought of franchise ownership but have realized that the current brand is not for you. While it can feel anticlimactic, trust your instincts, and start the process over again to make sure you find the right brand for you.

If you decide to move forward and sign a franchise agreement, you are on your way to becoming a business owner! The franchisor will send you the franchise agreement or a development agreement (if multiple units) to sign. The final steps are to review the legal obligations, make sure your financing is in order and move toward closing.

SUMMARY

Working with the franchisor should be a positive experience. It should be based on mutual interest and respect. The franchisor is not trying to sell you a used car. While the process may feel a little stilted due to the regulatory nature of it, staying professional and following the steps will allow you to compare and contrast multiple brands during your investigation.

- *Franchise Development Team.* You will be working with an internal or third-party franchise development representative that will guide you through the process. You should find this person helpful, informative, and understanding of your goals. If you have a terrible experience, that is not a good reflection of the brand.

- *Discovery Day.* You will likely be invited to visit the franchisor headquarters and experience the brand firsthand. This is a big commitment of time for both parties and is not a tire-kicking exercise. Only attend Discovery Day if you are 90 percent sure this is your brand. Similar to a final job interview, look for cultural fit and alignment.

- *Management Team.* Spend time with the founders, senior executives, and especially the direct support team that will work with you once you are a franchise owner. Visualize working with them on a daily basis and confirm this is a team with whom you can partner.

- *Franchisor Vision.* While it should not be considered a deal-breaker, it can be insightful to understand the organizational goals of the franchisor in the context of your personal and professional goals with the business.

- *Decision Time.* Expect to make a decision quickly after Discovery Day. If you have completed due diligence, validation, and Discovery Day and are paralyzed by the prospect of making a decision, you should revisit your motivations for starting the process and decide if the timing is right for you.

THE FRANCHISE
DISCLOSURE DOCUMENT

The best prophet of the
future is the past.

LORD BYRON

Once you have engaged with the franchisor and have established a mutual interest, it is likely they have sent you the Franchise Disclosure Document. This lengthy document, which can span over 100 pages, will be a primary source of research and due diligence for your investigation.

Commonly referred to as the FDD, this form is the legal disclosure document required by every franchisor to be filed at least annually with the Federal Trade Commission and individual states that have state-level regulations. Currently, there are 13 states that require additional filings in addition to the federal filing, such as California, New York, and Illinois.

The FDD gives you a wealth of information about the franchisor. The form and composition of the document are standardized for all franchisors and must include information on a variety of topics of interest to you. You'll see 23 sections or "Items" outlined in the form. Some parts of the FDD are general in nature, and other parts are more specific.

Below is a short explanation of each section. The sections and descriptions are current as of the date of this writing.

ITEM 1. *The Franchisor, any Parents, Predecessors, and Affiliates*

In this section, you will learn how long the franchisor has been in business and their complete history. You will learn about any specific laws that pertain to the industry and permits that may need to be acquired.

Experts say this item is vital to understanding who truly owns the franchise. It can reveal if the franchise is owned by a parent company, which is an essential consideration for prospective franchisees.

ITEM 2. *Business Experience*

This section will identify the key executives in the franchise and learn what role they play in the company.

Take note of the executives and founders, their business history and experience. You can find out loads of information with just a little internet searching on Google, LinkedIn, and other platforms.

ITEM 3. *Litigation*

Here you will learn if the company or any executives within the franchise have pending or past lawsuits. It is important to note the nature of the complaint and how it was resolved. Felonies listed include: fraud, violations of franchise law, unfair or deceptive practices / misrepresentation, and settled civil actions.

Although most quality franchises will go out of their way to avoid litigation, the simple fact that they have been sued should not preclude consideration of a brand by itself. Review the basis of any lawsuits, who initiated them and the outcomes.

Ultimately, if you see a pattern of lawsuits that are detrimental to system franchisees, you should strongly consider whether you want to associate with such a brand.

ITEM 4. *Bankruptcy*

You will see any bankruptcy filings within the past decade by the franchise or any key executive. Bankruptcies are not necessarily bad, but you should understand the context. It is essential to look into them to know why they were filed and ensure they are not part of a more significant issue within the franchise.

Bankruptcy information can be helpful in assessing the franchisor's financial stability and whether the company is capable of delivering the support it promises. You can also review this information in conjunction with Item 21, Financial Statements, to understand the financial health of the franchisor.

ITEM 5. *Initial Fees*

Here you will learn the investment necessary to purchase a franchise. Many of these costs must be covered before the doors of your business can open. It will lay out everything, including franchise fees, non-refundable fees, deposits, inventory fees, equipment fees, signage fees, and royalty fees.

It is easy to get discouraged when you begin reviewing fees. The franchisor is providing the system, processes, and support for you to run your business. But it is your business, and it costs money to start it. So make sure you are reviewing these items with a neutral eye. When you put your entire investment model together, these costs will make more sense as part of the bigger picture.

ITEM 6. *Other Fees*

This section helps you to understand the ongoing, expected costs associated with owning a franchise, including royalty, training, advertising, marketing, and software. Deadlines for these fees will also be disclosed.

Many of the fees outlined may not be in effect unless some event happens, such as a default. The possible items described in this section will vary widely among various franchise brands, so read each FDD carefully in this section if you are comparing ongoing fees.

ITEM 7. *Estimated Initial Investment*

By now, you understand that the initial franchise fee is only a small percentage of the costs associated with purchasing a franchise. This section will combine the total of the charges outlined above as well as other costs expected to get a franchise unit operational. The total is the dollar amount you'll be expected to invest if you were to choose to be a part of the company and should be based on the actual experience of other franchisees. It may be ranges or averages.

This Item will show each line item of significant expenditures in your initial investment. Each row will show two columns, a low amount and a high amount. In my experience, Item 7 can be very accurate for many line items because the costs are fixed, such as franchise fees, pre-negotiated equipment costs, furniture, fixtures, and other similar costs that are priced at a national level.

The most significant variable by far in this Item will be your leasehold improvements if your brand requires real estate. Candidates regularly ask why the investment range is so broad in Item 7, and I point them directly to this line item to review. The reality is that every single real estate deal is different and has different economics, even within the same shopping center. You may do far worse or far better than average in your real estate negotiations, so it pays to be conservative in your estimates as you review real estate costs.

One important note for Item 7 is that it will show something called Additional Funds, or working capital. The Federal Trade Commission requires that every franchisor show at least three months of working capital in this line item. It would be best if you did not base your estimate for working capital purely on this disclosure but instead based on your inquiries of actual franchisees during validation calls, as discussed in a later chapter.

ITEM 8. *Restrictions on Sources of Products and Services*

This section will outline if and where franchisees are required to purchase goods and services. Rules for non-approved products or services and alternative suppliers will be described here. Having required vendors helps to maintain consistency and quality across locations and may provide group buying power for the franchise system.

Other requirements, such as insurance, computer systems, or

software platforms, may also be discussed in this section.

ITEM 9. *Franchisee's Obligations*

This section is a table of contents for your principal obligations under the franchise and other agreements. It will help you find more detailed information about your responsibilities in these agreements and in sections of the FDD.

ITEM 10. *Financing*

Here the franchisor will explain if they offer any financing programs. These can range from loans to installment plans, to leasing arrangements. It is important to note that financing from a franchise is just like financing from a bank. If a franchisee defaults, the franchise agreement can be terminated.

Do not be surprised if this section simply states that the franchisor does not offer direct or indirect financing for any amount due under the franchise agreement. It may also affirm whether the franchisor will or will not guarantee any debt, lease, or other obligations.

ITEM 11. *Franchisor's Assistance, Advertising, Computer Systems and Training*

In this Item, the FDD breaks down the assistance and training new franchisees are provided to help them get started. It may also state that except for specific items listed, the franchisor is not required to provide you with any assistance.

Items that may be provided by the franchisor and outlined here include pre-opening assistance, site selection assistance, training, advertising, software, and marketing support.

ITEM 12. *Territory*

The territory in which you will be allowed to operate and where you are able to solicit customers is outlined here. You will learn whether each franchise has an assigned, protected territory or not. This is a very personal decision for each franchisee and is typically discussed in detail before attending Discovery Day.

Your specific market or territory will not be addressed directly in the FDD. You will negotiate your chosen territory location with the franchise development team during your investigation period, usually toward the end of the process.

ITEM 13. *Trademarks*

This section lists the trademarks, copyrights, patents, and proprietary information to which you will gain the rights under the franchise agreement. This section should be pretty straightforward.

Obviously, every brand will go to great lengths to protect their brand name and marks. You will have a license to use the marks but expect strong language about branding if you are in default of the franchise agreement.

ITEM 14. *Patents, Copyrights, Proprietary Information*

Similar to Item 13, this section lays out the patents and copyrights to which you gain access. It is valuable to review this section to understand the patents, copyrights, proprietary information, and patent restrictions for the franchise.

Expect strict language about intellectual property owned by the franchisor. This makes sense as they have worked very hard to build their brand. However, don't get overly concerned. The entire point of the franchise is for you to create a business based on their brand, so by following the system and working within the rules, you will be able to use all resources in any compelling way to run your business.

ITEM 15. *Obligation to Participate in the Operation of the Franchise Business*

Here you will learn the expectations of being a franchise owner. This can vary from franchise to franchise. Some expect you to manage the day-to-day operations, while others are fine with you hiring outside assistance. It will also outline whether the franchisee can participate in any other business ventures while under contract with the franchisor.

Many brands will have named positions you are required to fill to run your business, such as Franchise Owner, Operating Partner, or General Manager. Often multiple roles can be filled by a single person, such as the franchisee, but the system would still require someone to be named. This allows the system to standardize its systems, processes, and training, so that franchise locations are run in a consistent manner.

ITEM 16. *Restrictions on What the Franchisee May Sell*

As stated in Item 8, franchisors will both stipulate and limit what you must and can sell to maintain consistency across all locations. These restrictions should be expected, but it's important to review for anything unexpected.

It is likely you were drawn to the brand due to its proprietary products and services. If you come from the same industry, you should thoroughly review this section and consider if you are fine having little control over the product or service provided.

ITEM 17. *Renewal, Termination, Transfer and Dispute Resolution*

This Item details the procedure for renewing your franchise or exiting a franchise at the end of your agreement. The process for dispute resolution will also be outlined here.

If you have an attorney review the FDD and franchise agreement, review this section in detail and provide any questions to your attorney.

ITEM 18. *Public Figures*

If the franchise uses public figures in their advertising, the details of their relationship would be listed here.

ITEM 19. *Financial Performance Representations*

The structure of the FDD is pretty standardized throughout the whole document. However, the content of Item 19 is unique for each franchise, and it is allowed for it to be blank or exhaustive, or anything in between.

The FTC's Franchise Rule permits a franchisor to provide information about the actual or potential financial performance of its franchised and/or franchisor-owned outlets, if there is a reasonable basis for the information, and if the information is included in the disclosure document. Financial performance information that differs from that contained in Item 19 may be given only if: (1) a franchisor provides the actual records of an existing outlet you are considering buying; or (2) a franchisor supplements the information provided in this Item 19, for example, by providing information about possible performance at a particular location or under specific circumstances.

This is arguably the most critical section of the FDD. However, franchisors are not required to disclose information about potential income or sales. If they do, the law requires they have a reasonable basis for their claims. It is up to you to carefully examine this section and look for the following: figures from corporate stores, average sales, and earnings, gross sales, geographic difference, and the number of years the franchise has been in operation.

You should carefully review all of the FDD, but Item 19 cannot be missed and should be the basis of your financial projections and assumptions as you consider the franchise investment.

ITEM 20. *List of Franchise Outlets*

This is a listing that contains all the franchise locations that have opened, closed, or transferred in the past three years and the names of the franchise owners. Ideally, you see consistent growth. If you don't, you will want to look into why there wasn't growth over a specific time period by contacting franchise owners to understand any trends.

Take particular note of closures and the percentage of the entire system. Every franchise system will have underperforming units, but quality franchisors will step in to help those that are struggling to either improve their performance or assist them with a transfer. They want to avoid closures, so a high percentage of closures should be asked about during your investigation.

Once you receive the FDD, franchisors consider you in "validation" because you now have access to this listing of all franchisees in their system. While there are regulations about how and what the franchisor can share with you, there are no such restrictions on franchisees. Validation is an essential part of your due diligence, and the list here is where to start.

ITEM 21. *Financial Statements*

Here you will find important information about the company's financial status, including audited financial statements. This can showcase the overall health of the business, ideally showing steady growth and income from royalty payments as opposed to franchise sales.

The Federal Trade Commission requires a franchisor to submit audited financial statements, but usually only after the first two years. Genuinely understanding the franchisor's financial status can help you in your consideration of a significant investment. Ask your accountant to review these if you don't understand them.

ITEM 22. *Contracts*

These are the contracts you will be required to sign if you choose to open a franchise. Contracts include the franchise agreement along with other contracts that may include the following: development agreements, confidentiality agreements, leases, finance documents, purchase agreements, service agreements, general release, software agreements, bank draft authorizations, and promissory notes. Be sure to review these documents with a franchise attorney.

ITEM 23. *Receipt*

You must read and review the FDD at least 14 days prior to signing a franchise agreement. This section acknowledges that you received the FDD. Both you and the franchisor should sign this receipt, although it does not obligate you to anything.

KEY SECTIONS OF THE FDD

Getting through the FDD can seem tedious, and I have had many candidates shortcut or skip a thorough review of this vital document. Choose a time when you are focused and have no distractions, like maybe a weekend morning with a cup of coffee. Read through the entire document and make notes of any questions to ask the franchisor.

Much of the more detailed requirements and obligations will be in the franchise agreement, so if you have any experience reviewing or negotiating agreements, you can spend extra time studying the franchise agreement directly. The FDD is designed to convey this information in a more readable format. Of course, as discussed elsewhere, it is always good advice to hire a franchise attorney to review the documents for anything you don't understand.

The key sections you absolutely should not omit are Items 1-4, 7, and 19-21. The most critical financial parts are Item 7, Estimated Initial Investment, and Item 19, Financial Performance Representations. Most candidates will want to go first to Item 19 to understand the financials to help be efficient in their review of the opportunity.

Typically, there is also a series of exhibits to the FDD. These can provide supporting information for the 23 Items listed above. The most critical exhibit usually included in the FDD is the franchise agreement you will sign if you become a franchisee. Financial statements for the franchisor are also included if required.

The FDD is the most comprehensive and official source of information you will have on the franchise opportunity. Make sure to spend as much time as needed to understand the document fully before signing a franchise agreement.

SUMMARY

The Franchise Disclosure Document, or FDD, is a critical piece of official information. All franchises are required to file an FDD annually with the Federal Trade Commission and a handful of registration states.

You must carefully review the FDD, which has 23 sections or "Items," plus the attached exhibits, including the franchise agreement.

- *Key Sections.* The key sections you absolutely should not omit are Items 1-4, 7, and 19-21. The most critical financial parts are Item 7, Estimated Initial Investment, and Item 19, Financial Performance Representations.

- *Exhibits.* The most critical exhibit usually included in the FDD is the franchise agreement you will sign if you become a franchisee. Financial statements for the franchisor are also included if required.

- *Importance.* Because it is the most important piece of information you will receive from the franchisor, you need to spend as much time as necessary to fully understand the FDD.

VALIDATION: TALKING WITH OTHER FRANCHISEES

Trust, but verify.

RONALD REAGAN

I f there is one step you cannot miss during your due diligence investigations for a franchise, it is validation. This is where you will call and talk with as many existing and former franchisees as you have time for. You will confirm their experiences and compare how they match up with the information in the FDD and what the franchisor has told you.

While validation is an essential part of any franchise investigation, it is an absolute requirement for certain franchise brands. These include brands without an Item 19 disclosure in their FDD, brands that are just launching, and brands that are the first in their industry. The importance of substantial discussions on the experience of franchisees in any system cannot be overstated.

MAKING VALIDATION CALLS

A good percentage of candidates avoid or dislike the process of validation calls. It can be time-consuming and sometimes frustrating, trying to reach and talk to people. It can also feel intrusive. However, it is an essential part of your due diligence. Don't get overwhelmed. Follow the process, and you will find this the most valuable part of your research. All the franchisees you talk to also went through this process and likely validated with multiple franchisees, so they should be more inclined to pay it forward and help you with validation.

The purpose of these calls is to confirm the information the franchisor should have already shared with you. No franchise is perfect. What you are trying to find out are the key factors of success and challenges for each system and how that fits with your skills, experience, and capital position.

No one knows the business like those out in the field. Provided you build the proper rapport, they're likely to give you candid answers to your questions, in turn helping you decide if the opportunity is right for you.

You will want to speak with several franchisees, preferably some of whom are very successful and some who are reaping average returns or even struggling. By reviewing the responses and comparing your own management style and market geography to those currently operating stores, you'll gain a better idea of where you might end up if you purchase this franchise.

One thing to keep in mind: at any given time, there will be several people researching franchise opportunities, and a franchisor's more successful franchisees must field a number of these calls. Have a clear agenda to keep your conversation organized and on topic, aiding both you and the franchisee. Some new brands with only a few franchisees will invariably have group validation calls. This is simply the only reasonable way their small number of franchisees can handle the influx of incoming validation calls.

EXPECTATIONS FOR VALIDATION

They call them "validation" calls for a reason—you are validating and confirming the information the franchisor should have already shared with you. There are several considerations for how to approach these calls for a better experience.

- *No Perfection.* No franchise is perfect. What you are trying to find out is what are the critical factors of success and challenges for each system and how that fits with your skills, experience, and capital position.
- *Franchisor Guidance.* The franchisor may likely provide a shortlist of franchisees they suggest you call. Don't be surprised if these are the top-performing locations in the system. This is a good thing, and you should speak with franchisees that are the best representation of the brand. Speaking with failed franchisees can be OK if taken in context but also has pitfalls. The successful franchisees will share plenty of challenges and will be your best source of information.
- *Group Calls.* For efficiency, many brands, and in particular younger brands, may hold group validation calls on a weekly

basis. If the company only has 20-30 franchisees, then the same people are getting bombarded with validation calls weekly, so don't feel the group calls are a bad thing. It is merely courteous and more respectful to the franchisees that are trying to run their businesses. Even though it is a group, don't hesitate to ask your more burning questions. And ask if there are individual franchisees willing to talk more separately.

- *Open-Ended Questions.* Rather than ask yes or no questions, ask open-ended questions to get the franchisees to expand. For example, instead of "Are you happy with the system?" you might ask, "How do you feel about where you are now compared to where you thought you would be?"
- *Mutual Fit.* The franchisor will award you a franchise if they feel you are a good fit with skills/experience/culture. Like a job interview, it can be somewhat subjective. As you talk with other franchisees, you may start to get a feel for the culture of the people in that system. Trust your instincts about culture and fit. This should be a primary role of Discovery Day, but getting to know many franchisees will also help you make this last subjective decision.

TOPICS FOR FRANCHISEE VALIDATION

The following list covers the most critical areas you will want to cover during your calls with existing franchisees:

- *Franchisor/Franchisee Relations.* How do the franchisees feel about their relationship with the franchise company?

Are they getting the support they want and need? Do they think the franchisor cares about their success and is willing to help them as needed? A good franchise company will work continuously to keep its current franchisees happy, and open communication is paramount. If most franchisees feel good about the franchisor, it's a sign the company is supportive, caring, and focused on the success of its franchisees.

- *Training.* Ideally, the training a new franchisee receives should prepare them to open and run the business. If you hear from franchisees that they were unprepared to open, you might assume the training program was inadequate. Be sure you understand the critical elements necessary for success and how the franchisor will help provide these elements before you become involved.

- *General Support.* You should expect to get a glowing report on the overall support provided to franchisees by a franchisor. This support should include helping the franchisees resolve any problems that arise and providing ongoing training as needed. A franchisor should also be responsive to changes in the marketplace, so you'll want to gauge the comments of franchisees about how innovations or modifications to the system are integrated.

- *Opening Support.* A franchise company can truly shine when it provides superior support to the new franchisee during the opening of the business. Ask the existing franchisees if they received assistance in site selection, lease negotiations, buildout, the permitting processes, or any other areas unique to the opening of the business.

- *Marketing Programs.* Weekly, monthly, or annual marketing programs, social media support, graphics, pricing, and packaging are all important topics to understand in any franchise system. You won't make a profit if you don't have customers, and for that reason, most franchisors collect marketing dollars from each of their franchisees and spend the combined amount on promoting brand awareness on a large scale. Being part of a well-known brand is a significant advantage of a franchise system and usually worth the money spent. Find out how the existing franchisees feel about the way their money is spent, but beware: This is the one area you are most likely to find complaints, as every franchisee considers him or herself a marketing expert. Balancing all feedback is essential here.

- *Initial and Ongoing Investment.* Before calling any franchisee, you should have read the franchisor's Franchise Disclosure Document (FDD), which in Item 7 will give you a wide range for the total initial investment required for opening this business. You can get a better feel for the investment needed by talking to the franchisees and learning how much they invested. Even more importantly, you can learn what they would do differently if they could do it over again. This is an excellent question for franchisees who operate in markets like yours, as you can get a better idea of the costs you will face in opening your franchise.

- *Purchasing Power.* This is another massive advantage of being part of a franchise system, so be sure to find out if the franchisor uses the collective buying power of the total system to get discounted pricing on equipment and inventory. Be sure to ask if these savings are passed through to the franchisees. If there are rebates to the franchisor from vendors, don't be alarmed, as they should still be negotiating great national discounts for their system franchisees. However, it pays to verify.

- **Earnings or EBITDA.** Everyone's favorite subject, the discussion of earnings or EBITDA (Earnings Before Interest, Taxes, Depreciation or Amortization) between a franchisor and a potential franchisee is strictly regulated. But there is no such restriction when talking with system franchisees. While you can often find earnings information in Item 19 of the FDD, it may only include company-owned locations, system averages, only revenue information, or otherwise limited information. If it's an emerging brand, there may not be enough history to have a robust Item 19. Thus, your best source of earnings information is from the current franchisees.

  With hope, by the time you get to this issue, you'll have developed a relationship with the franchisee, making it comfortable to ask questions such as, "How long were you open before you showed a profit?" and "What is your typical net profit per month?" You can also glean valuable earnings information by talking about the average number of customers, average ticket or invoice amounts, and even the average number of calls or visits per sale.

  If you don't get a clear idea of what a typical unit earns, do not proceed with the purchase. You are not interested in franchising because you want to be surprised; you are buying a franchise because of the *proven and provable* value of the franchisor's system.

- *How to Fail.* One of my colleagues introduced me to this concept, and it's my favorite question. This sounds like an unusual query, but it's one of the best topics to pose to a franchisee in any system. By now, you should have prepared a financial projection for the franchise and know how to build appropriate revenue. While it's easy to confirm your projections with existing franchisees, this question will force the franchisee to consider the one critical skill, strategy, or experience needed to be successful in the system. It's a valuable question that provides clarity.

Besides talking to current franchisees, you may want to talk to some former franchisees. You will find the contact information of any franchisee that has left the system in the past year in the FDD. You will want to find out why they left and what kind of experience they had.

In some cases, franchisees will have left for personal reasons or perhaps because they found the opportunity wasn't right for them. If you compare the responses of these people to those of the successful franchisees, you may be able to see a trend that will help you determine if:

1) You identify with one group more than the other; and

2) If the success or failure of a franchisee is due more to the personality and experience of the franchisee or the support and system of the franchisor.

Your satisfaction and happiness as a franchisee often depend not only on your success but on the overall culture of the franchise system. By talking to current franchisees, you will learn the answers to many questions and find out if you would fit in with the franchisees. These people will be your peers and are valuable resources to you as you build your business.

SUMMARY

Validation is one of the most essential components of your due diligence. Building rapport and speaking with franchisees in a system is paramount to gathering the critical information you need to make a decision. There are multiple vital considerations for the validation process.

- *Making Validation Calls.* Approach the process with a positive attitude and follow the recommendations of the franchisor while contacting as many franchisees as needed to answer your most pressing questions.

- *Expectations for Validation.* No franchise is perfect. Find similar markets to call, stick to your process, and be balanced in your approach. Every franchisee went through the same process as you, so be gracious and respectful, and you will find plenty of franchisees who are happy to share their experience.

- *Topics for Franchisee Validation.* Do research on the most critical areas of support and interaction with the franchisor, such as topics covered in this chapter, and address those during your validation calls.

SIGNING THE FRANCHISE AGREEMENT

Once you complete Discovery Day, the franchisor will expect a pretty quick answer to the question of whether you are in or out. Based on your affirmative answer, they will send you an executable version of the franchise agreement. By signing the franchise agreement and paying the franchise fee, you will become a franchisee. This is worth a small celebration! Stop, take a breath, and congratulate yourself for acting to achieve your future vision. You closed the gap of anxiety through confidence in yourself.

Nearly all franchise agreements are 10 years long. At the end of 10 years, there will be an option for both parties to review the past decade and agree to stay partners or terminate. If you are a solid performer and not in default, there should be no reason a franchisor wouldn't want to extend with you. There's usually an extension fee of some sort, most likely to cover legal and review expenses. If you are successful and seek to renew your agreement, these fees will seem nominal, often ranging from $5,000 to $10,000.

As you consider signing the franchise agreement, you will likely learn that franchisors rarely, if ever, negotiate the franchise agreement. Trying to use an attorney to extract concessions may lead to frustration. It could possibly even crater your business deal altogether. Items that are unique to you as a franchisee, such as territory, credit, or timeline, may allow some room for negotiation, as they are usually addressed in addendums to the franchise agreement. Consult a franchise attorney if you have any questions on this topic.

Once you sign the franchise agreement and pay the franchise fee(s), you are officially a franchisee and ready to begin training to open your business. Your franchisor will provide a specific process to follow to onboard you and launch your business. Don't worry about knowing what to do; this is the point of a franchise!

DO I NEED AN ATTORNEY?

It's natural to be anxious about making a substantial commitment of time and money. You want to be perfectly clear on your rights and obligations in the franchise agreement. Whether to hire an attorney is a common question. If so, who do you choose?

I would never advise a candidate to forego hiring an attorney to assist them. However, I recommend that candidates need to understand a few essential characteristics of a franchise agreement.

- *Negotiability (or Lack Thereof).* First, expect the basic franchise agreement may be non-negotiable. The actual language in the franchise agreement attached as an Exhibit to the FDD will nearly always be what you sign; I have never seen one negotiated yet. When you consider this, it makes sense. If every franchisee were getting a different deal, brand consistency would collapse. If you believe in the brand and management team, you should be happy they will not negotiate the franchise agreement, as it protects you from wayward franchisees going off-brand. However, you should consult an attorney if you have any doubts and again, I would never advise against seeking the advice of a qualified franchise attorney.

- **Addendums.** While the basic franchise agreement is hardly ever negotiated, there are some negotiable terms, usually added as exhibits or addendums to the agreement, which can often be negotiated. These are items exclusive to you as a franchisee. The most essential topics you will negotiate with the franchisor include:

  - *Territory.* All franchisors set territory differently depending on their business model. Some territories are strictly defined by the franchisor, and some are more loosely negotiated. Territory could be determined by population, the number of businesses, or other factors. In general, the goal is to give each territory relatively equal revenue potential.

  - *Credit.* Your personal guaranty, your spouse's guaranty, and other terms regarding your credit position are unique to you and separately negotiated. Like other creditors, franchisors will ask for security to bring leverage to them in the agreement. This usually comes in the form of a personal guaranty.

I did not hire an attorney when I signed my franchise agreements. However, I spent my career negotiating transactions, bank loans, acquisitions, and other business contracts. Knowing in advance the franchisor would not negotiate the agreement, I reviewed, understood, and accepted the terms, and then moved on. Like a bank loan or mortgage, the deal is one-sided but generally based on a relationship. Franchisors have often been known to make special concessions for franchisees in case of hardship, untimely death, or other unforeseen circumstances.

If you cannot understand the FDD or franchise agreement, or have any doubts about signing a franchise agreement, I highly advise you to hire an attorney, particularly one who specializes in franchising or works in the space on a regular basis. Corporate attorneys unfamiliar with franchising may believe everything is negotiable, and they may cause you headaches and substantial fees by trying to change the terms in the franchise agreement.

While franchise agreements can be onerous and feel one-sided, good franchisors go to great extremes to avoid litigation. They particularly seek to avoid initiating litigation against franchisees. If you are following the system and not sabotaging the brand, they are likely to work with you on any issues you may have. All litigation must be disclosed in the FDD Item 3, and any good franchisor will want to avoid disclosing any sort of litigation.

These days, franchise agreements are typically sent in electronic format to be signed digitally with confirmed copies for you and the franchisor. Don't be alarmed by this; it is all perfectly legal and enforceable. If you have bought a house in recent years, you know that high volume transaction documents are now mostly electronic.

REVIEW VS. NEGOTIATION

Most franchise attorneys will advise you that it will be difficult or impossible to negotiate the franchise agreement. For that reason, they should offer to perform a review of the FDD and franchise agreement, and give you a breakdown of your risks, rights, and obligations under the contract. This can give you significant peace of mind if you have deep concerns about the franchise agreement.

A review is different from hiring an attorney to attempt to negotiate and extract concessions from the franchisor. A review will outline your rights and obligations in explanatory form but will not attempt to engage the franchisor in negotiations.

While it is tempting to try to negotiate the franchise agreement, it is also important to manage your expectations. I strongly recommend you engage a specialized franchise attorney who can advise you on the potential fees and probable success in negotiating the franchise agreement.

SIGNING THE AGREEMENT

Once you have signed the franchise agreement and any related documents, it's time to take a breath and celebrate! Having spent many hours over the previous weeks contemplating this huge step, you may not realize the emotional release you need. Yes, it can be scary, but it is also exhilarating to sign a franchise agreement and become a business owner. Take time to pause and enjoy the moment. There will be plenty of time to worry about training, real estate, and the next steps.

Holding a closing dinner or small celebratory event can be an excellent way to mark the milestone and set your course into business ownership. It can also signal to family and friends that you have made a transition, and they should now identify you as a business owner. You're an entrepreneur! Enjoy the moment, as only a small fraction of people who consider franchise ownership end up moving forward.

SUMMARY

Signing the franchise agreement is both an exciting and anxious moment. Once you complete Discovery Day, the franchisor will shortly expect you to sign the franchise agreement or will move on to other candidates.

- *Do I Need an Attorney?* It is always recommended to consult an attorney if you have any concerns about the franchise agreement. Because this is a long-term commitment with significant financial implications, hiring an attorney can give you peace of mind.
- *Review vs. Negotiation.* Be aware that it may be difficult or impossible to get concessions in the franchise agreement. Most franchise attorneys will offer a review of the FDD and franchise agreement for a reasonable amount to explain your rights and obligations. Consult a franchise attorney to advise you on the probability of success and potential fees in negotiating the franchise agreement.
- *Signing the Agreement.* There is a lot of effort and emotion leading up to signing the franchise agreement. Enjoy the

moment and celebrate your transition to being a business owner. There will be plenty of time to get started with training and operations, and your franchisor will have all the steps to get you started.

10

FINANCING
YOUR FRANCHISE

> Whatever the mind of man can conceive
> and believe, it can achieve.
>
> NAPOLEON HILL

You are excited about taking the next step and moving forward to start your own franchise business. But how do you finance this investment?

There are many ways entrepreneurs finance their franchise investments. You need to fully understand your current and projected capital position before you sign a franchise agreement. I have had candidates with widely varying views on this. Some want to minimize their cash investment and maximize positive leverage, borrowing as much as possible. Other candidates who are debt- and risk-averse want to avoid borrowing or being in debt. You can undoubtedly choose the path you are comfortable with, but you need to understand the risks and rewards attached to various financing options.

Carefully consider your risk profile, working capital needs, and future expansion plans before making a financing decision. Most franchisees will combine two or more sources of capital when starting a franchise. In many cases, the financing sources available to you can strongly influence your choice of a franchise brand. For example, while most franchises have SBA-guaranteed loans available, specific categories of franchises, such as salon suites or businesses with no employees, may not be eligible for SBA financing, forcing you to consider other options.

I have found that many prospective franchise owners are not aware of the wide variety of capital sources available to them. Although cash, 401k rollovers, and SBA-guaranteed loans are most common, there are many other methods that can help achieve your goals, whether they're maximizing leverage, reducing risk, or creating a stable income.

CASH ON HAND

This is the safest, lowest risk, and the most common way people finance their franchise investment. By using idle cash, they can avoid interest costs and debt-service risks while putting their capital to work.

Most of my candidates utilize liquid cash along with another financing method, such as the ones listed below.

REAL WORLD EXAMPLE

Tom was a partner in his family-owned business. He had a high net worth and liquid cash, but he had multiple children who likely would not carry on in the family business. His goal was to create a franchise company that he did not share with his siblings so he would have retirement income and a company for his children to work and manage in the future. Because he had a high current income and excess cash, he used part of his liquid funds to get the company started and diversify away from his family's business.

SELLING LIQUID SECURITIES

Many long-working corporate executives find their entire net worth is tied up in the stock market. If they've been successful as a corporate employee, they've maxed their 401k plans and invested their after-tax cash in liquid securities such as stocks and bonds.

I've had multiple candidates in this situation. Suddenly, they realize their entire financial future is dependent on Wall Street and geopolitical events due to their overexposure to the financial markets. They see moving a portion or in some cases all, of their net worth into a business they control. Yes, there are risks, but with the many ups and downs of the stock market over the last 20 to 30 years, this is one way candidates decide to take more control of their financial future.

REAL WORLD EXAMPLE

Ellen was a senior executive with a large public company. Through stock options over the years, she had accumulated a significant concentration in a single company stock investment—her employer. Ellen chose to sell a portion of her company stock to diversify and invest in her new franchise business. With the proceeds, she funded all cash for the first franchise location, allowing her to secure debt financing for the second location more quickly.

PORTFOLIO LOANS

Some franchisees with large securities portfolios find that instead of selling the securities and creating possible taxable gains, they can borrow against their portfolios without liquidating them and get low interest rates. Most banks or brokerages are pleased to provide portfolio loans at a low cost to investors. There are no restrictions on how you use the loan proceeds.

I've had several candidates with large securities portfolios who have lines of credit available to them through their brokerage firm. Otherwise called margin loans, because these loans are backed by immediately liquid securities, the interest rates can be much lower than any other type of loan. The risk is if the stock market crashed and you had borrowed the maximum, you might have to repay the loan up to the amount of decreased value in your securities. Speak to your investment advisor to consider this type of financing.

REAL WORLD EXAMPLE

Elizabeth was an executive with a large publicly traded consumer products company. She had built up a significant portfolio of company stock in her employer and felt she was too concentrated in one investment. As she considered investing in a franchise business, she decided to liquidate part of her portfolio concentrated in her employer's stock to diversify and invest in her own business.

HOME EQUITY LINE OF CREDIT

For the average American, their home is usually their most significant asset. A home equity line of credit, or HELOC, is a popular way for potential franchisees to finance their business investment. This is usually in the form of a second mortgage on your primary residence that can tap the unutilized equity in your home to put into your business. There are no restrictions on how you use the loan proceeds, and the interest can be tax-deductible. Consult with a tax professional to determine if it would be deductible in your situation.

One of my candidates had inherited a house and had no debt on it, but she had plenty of current income from her executive position to pay a mortgage while she started a semi-absentee beauty franchise. For her, getting a HELOC at a low interest rate with no closing costs was a quick and easy way to raise the cash necessary to start her business without liquidating other investments or reducing her family's lifestyle.

REAL WORLD EXAMPLE

Rob and Harriet lived in a lovely home in the suburbs they had inherited from Rob's parents. They decided to tap their home equity via a HELOC to fund their startup in a painting franchise. They liked that it had no closing costs or fees and a low interest rate, and it could be paid off and borrowed on again later if they had a short term need for working capital. It was a perfect solution for them.

401K OR IRA ROLLOVER

Also called ROBS (Rollover for Business Startups), this IRS-approved method will roll over all or a portion of your current IRA or 401k balance into a new qualified plan that invests in your company's stock instead of the broader market or mutual funds.

This is a common and accessible way for franchisees to diversify their investments and start a franchise without debt. You will need to work with a specialized custodian to complete this method, but several quality national providers work exclusively in franchising.

A recent survey study by Guidant Financial found that this method of financing a franchise investment was the most popular method. A high percentage of my candidates will utilize this method for a portion or all of their total franchise investment.

REAL WORLD EXAMPLE

Bob was in career transition and considering franchises. He had a $1.2 million 401k balance from many years in corporate America, but his spouse did not work, and he had school-age children. Bob needed to produce income pretty quickly. He chose to invest $500,000 of his 401k balance in a semi-absentee salon suites franchise rather than borrow, which allowed him to avoid debt-service payments and helped cash flow while he pursued a new corporate position.

SBA-GUARANTEED LOAN

Most banks have loan programs that will loan to small business entrepreneurs with a guaranty from the U.S. Small Business Administration (SBA). The SBA does not loan money but rather guarantees bank loans on behalf of small business owners. For beginning franchisees, they will typically be using what is called an SBA 7(a) program loan.

Many franchises are already registered with the SBA, making loans easier and quicker to get approved. SBA loans are typically easier to get approved than a conventional loan due to the government guarantee, although there is a lot of paperwork and meaningful fees involved.

While the SBA has certain limits and requirements for the loans, there is plenty of variability in the terms you may receive from different banks, so it pays to shop around if you are seeking an SBA loan.

I utilized an SBA-guaranteed bank loan along with cash to finance my first franchise purchase, and I have found a high percentage of candidates use this method. There are fees and paperwork involved, but it's a very viable and available source of funding.

REAL WORLD EXAMPLE

Daphne bought a three-unit territory in a fitness franchise with a total cost of $375,000 to purchase three territory rights and open the first unit. She chose to get qualified for an SBA-guaranteed Section 7(a) bank loan and received excellent terms, including six months' interest only and a low interest rate from a local bank. She was approved for an 80 percent loan of the total cost. She put $75,000 saved cash into the investment and borrowed $300,000 under the SBA loan.

PARTNERS

Many franchisees have friends, family members, or business acquaintances who are looking for business investment opportunities. There are many variables and business terms to consider before taking on a partner, and you'll want to explore the legal ramifications as well. But if an appropriate partnership agreement outlining control, exit strategies, duties, and obligations of each partner is completed, this can be another possible way to fund your growth.

> **REAL WORLD EXAMPLE**
>
> *Drew, Gordon, and Brian were successful sales reps in the same financial services business. They shared a common goal to build passive income streams and work their way out of corporate America. They decided to pool their capital to open multiple units in a shared office suites franchise that had few employees and allowed them to continue in their current positions while rolling out locations by buying the rights to their entire market. This allowed them to scale and diversify risk across multiple locations.*

FRANCHISOR-ARRANGED FINANCING

Depending on the type of franchise and cost of buildout or equipment, the franchisor may have financing programs in-house or with a closely-aligned program lender. This can often be the most attractive source of funding, especially if no personal collateral is required.

One of the franchises we work with is in the residential tree service business. They have an agreement with a financing company to provide equipment financing to all franchisees that meet the minimum credit requirements. The financing company gets captive customers while the franchise can roll out its units faster and help franchisees negotiate better financing rates.

> **REAL WORLD EXAMPLE**
>
> *In my indoor cycling fitness franchise, I decided to lease my 50 stationary bikes through a special lease from a vendor arranged by my franchisor. It allowed me to free up my SBA loan for other needs and increase working capital.*

ALTERNATIVE LENDERS

There are several specialty lenders that have programs for equipment or other asset-backed or unsecured loans. While these are not ubiquitous, there are quality loan brokers who can source and identify financing to meet your specific needs.

> **REAL WORLD EXAMPLE**
>
> Doug and Gerry wanted to invest in multiple salon suite franchise locations. Each put in 20 percent of the total investment, and they wanted to borrow the rest. However, this category of franchises does not qualify for the SBA 7(a) program, so they borrowed 60 percent of the costs from an alternative lending company that provides third-party financing with no collateral requirements. This allowed them to avoid pledging personal assets while getting similar loan terms to an SBA-guaranteed bank loan.

MULTIPLE UNIT STRATEGIES

The majority of franchise placements are for multiple units or territories. Candidates want to reserve territory and have the rights to future expansion in their market. This is very common among my candidates but should prompt you to consider your financing strategy carefully.

For example, the SBA will guarantee multiple loans up to a combined $5.0 million for one borrower. However, most banks with whom you secure an SBA loan will likely not loan to open a second location until your first location has been open 12 months and is cash-flow positive. Thus, a strategy might be to open the first location with a 401k rollover or all cash, which would allow the second unit to be opened sooner with bank financing and higher leverage. In short, if you're seeking to open multiple units of a franchise, your strategy should be customized to your situation.

SPEAK WITH AN EXPERT

Whether using any of the above strategies, some combination of providers, or other sources, financing your franchise investment is a huge decision and should not be taken lightly. Many candidates find the available financing options may help them decide between two finalist franchises in consideration. When in doubt, talk to experienced franchise lenders to understand your options. If you have a franchise consultant, they can refer you to the premier national franchise financing providers.

SUMMARY

Financing your franchise is one of the most critical considerations in the due diligence process. You should consider learning about your financing options or even getting preapproved ahead of franchise signing.

The financing options available to you may help direct your choice of industry or brand. For example, the SBA may decide it will not guarantee bank loans for your chosen franchise category. Or, if you want to open multiple units, it may require a more considered financing strategy.

There are many options available, and most new franchisees will use a combination of financing strategies that fit their goals. Some of the financing options available include:

- Cash on Hand
- Selling Liquid Securities
- Portfolio Loans
- Home Equity Line of Credit
- 401k or IRA Rollover
- SBA Guaranteed Loan
- Partners
- Franchisor-Arranged Financing
- Alternative Lenders

In addition to choosing your preferred financing source, other factors, such as seeking to open multiple units, will require a more formulated strategy. Speak to a franchise financing expert early in your process to get a full understanding of your options for your chosen category or brand.

11

FEAR, ANXIETY, AND ROADBLOCKS

Inaction breeds doubt and fear. Action breeds confidence and courage. If you want to conquer fear, do not sit home and think about it. Go out and get busy.

DALE CARNEGIE

Fear is the one thing that can stop your entrepreneurial journey dead in its tracks. Even after starting a business, controlling fear will need to be part of your arsenal. It reminds me of my own experience in launching our business.

Due to the inevitable delays in the real estate process, the opening for our fitness franchise was pushed back into spring. Heading into summer is not the optimal time to launch a fitness business in the Midwest. In addition, the franchise had recently made a change in the business model, moving from class packages to a recurring membership focus, which had a dampening effect on grand opening revenue.

Thus, our launch was not the record-breaking success we

had heard about from other studios. As we moved into summer and fall, we were a little further behind our pro forma than I had projected. As fear started creeping in, I had a few sleepless nights wondering if we would be able to meet our projections.

My anxiety continued for a few weeks until I realized that my inaction was breeding the fear. When I calmed down and focused, I made a list of my biggest obstacles and opportunities. We installed a new sales process, and I talked to a few creditors, asking for small deferrals as we continued to ramp up. Just a couple of discussions and minor adjustments with two parties solved our short-lived issue until the new year hit, and our improved revenue launched us past break even. Every business owner will go through obstacles. Keeping perspective around those challenges is crucial. While I experienced a massive sigh of relief when we hit our first-year goals, to the other parties involved, it was all business as usual. I realized then that my anxiety was more rooted in fear, pride, and ego than any fundamental business problem. Once I looked at things objectively, solutions presented themselves, and we moved forward successfully.

Having the confidence in yourself to handle future unknown problems is really the solution to fear, which may be the biggest hurdle you will face in starting a franchise business.

SIGNING THE FRANCHISE AGREEMENT

I tell my candidates to break down their fear and isolate each question so we can focus on the real issues. It is human nature to fill a void or question with an answer if we don't have one. Similar to the first time you ride a bike as a child, it all seems so scary, and those unknowns quickly get filled in with speculation and worst-case scenarios. But once you get your legs going, you realize it's just a different feeling and skill you needed to master.

While it's important to assess your risk, you can easily talk yourself out of any business investment. There are plenty of reasons why you shouldn't take the leap. It's essential to seek out the reasons why it does make sense and remember why you started this journey in the first place. Do you remember your emotional trigger?

If the fear is you won't be profitable, talk to 20 franchisees in your prospective franchise system. If 20 out of 20 say they are profitable, that will go a long way toward assuaging that fear. Or if 19 out of 20 say it took them nine months to break even, then you probably should be considering a minimum of nine months of working capital into your budget.

If the fear is you won't be able to find quality staff, then again, validation and due diligence can address that fear: Talk with enough franchisees to make you comfortable that good staff are out there for you. Ask for case studies and experiences; that's part of the benefit of a franchise.

Ultimately, I tell candidates that even with perfect due diligence and validation, one can only get to a 95 percent confidence level. Never 100 percent. You have to bridge that last percentage gain through confidence in yourself, believing that you will do whatever it takes not to fail and solve every problem thrown your way. Accepting that you can't have all the answers before jumping in is an important step to getting over the fear factor as well.

Tom was excited by the prospect of a new franchise brand, carving out a niche within the health and beauty market. But he was fearful that he would not be able to run it effectively while keeping his current corporate position. Through validation, he spoke with numerous franchisees in that system who had successful businesses run by a manager while they pursued other careers or interests. This reduced his fear and allowed him to move ahead with franchise signing for an exciting new brand.

YOUR SPOUSE

This point cannot be overstated: if your spouse is not on board with you starting a new business, the process will fail. If you are in transition and would like to consider franchise ownership, you need to inform yourself first then get through it with your spouse in a logical and non-emotional way. There is often a high degree of concern by the spouse about the perceived risks of starting a business. Getting emotional about it will only create a roadblock.

While I am no marriage counselor, I have found that open and honest communication between spouses is a requirement for serious consideration of starting a franchise. Even if you have lots of wealth, we all have various preconceived notions about what a franchise business is or have heard stories good and bad about other people that tried to open a business. These biases form a protective barrier in our decision-making and often prevent us from making otherwise rational decisions.

I decided to treat my wife like any other investor, and I pitch her on any business ideas. I create a PowerPoint slide deck with all relevant information, due diligence, etc. then schedule time away from the family so we can have a business discussion. This method can help the less-involved spouse feel engaged in the decision-making process, and it may help create a supportive partner in your new venture. You will need that support as you traverse the unknowns of starting a new business. Make it a priority to form a consensus with your spouse, including decisions on investment level, industry, employee type, and the franchisee role required for the brand.

FRIENDS AND FAMILY

Your friends and family can have a significant impact on your decision to move forward with a franchise. For instance, if your spouse isn't on board, then it's really a non-starter. But expanding beyond your spouse to garner support from other family members can be also be an important factor to many people.

Most of your close friends and especially your family may question why you would take any risk in starting a new business. They may ask you why you don't just get a new job. If this is the case, they clearly don't understand your motivational trigger.

Once you are in due diligence with several brands, expect to receive everyone's opinion as a consumer of that product or service. Whatever their bias is toward that particular brand, service, or category, it's certainly not based on actual due diligence, research, and validation, all of which you have completed in your process. Trust your instincts. While you love and respect your family and friends, it's not their journey. If you decided to run a marathon, which very few people statistically ever accomplish, you likely wouldn't take training advice from family and friends who never exercise.

PROFESSIONAL ADVISORS

Most of us have professional advisors upon whom we rely to help us with things like taxes, bookkeeping, investments, and the like. As a fundamental premise of their role, these advisors either expressly or implicitly consider themselves fiduciaries for you. This means it's their job to educate you and protect you from harm. Their bias will be to explain to you about all the risks and possible ways you might fail, but talk very little about the rewards if you succeed. So, if you need financial advice, consider a neutral third party who can give you objective advice on a transactional basis.

I have seen instances where investment advisors work hard to talk candidates out of a franchise business investment. If they are paid an asset-based fee, which most are these days, then removing assets from their care to invest in a business has a harmful effect on their revenue. Be aware of a potential conflict of interest in receiving business advice from an investment professional.

Your accountant or CPA may not have a direct revenue interest in your decision to start a business (indeed, an accountant may get more business from such an investment), but if you have a long-standing relationship with them, they may still be more conservative in their advice. If they are helping you complete projections and pro formas, then their advice should hold more weight.

Finally, some of my very closest friends are high-quality attorneys. However, I have never met an attorney without a strong opinion on almost every topic. While we cover working with attorneys in another chapter, understand that most corporate attorneys spend their entire careers contemplating doomsday scenarios and protecting their clients from them. While I would never advise going without legal advice if you want it, be aware that without deeply understanding the business model, no professional is likely in a position to give you business advice on a franchise business.

> **REAL WORLD EXAMPLE**
>
> Linda was contemplating starting a franchise business in the home healthcare field. Her brother-in-law was a litigation attorney and suggested to her that the liability exposure was too high, although he had not reviewed the FDD or talked with the franchisor about its extensive and customized insurance policy, which was available and modeled into the expenses for every franchisee. Once Linda hired an attorney to review the FDD and franchise agreement and assess her risk exposure, she found the franchisor had more than adequate risk management structures in place.

SUMMARY

It can be anxiety-producing to step into business ownership and sign a franchise agreement. We are hard-wired as humans for fear to drive our decision-making. This can be a good thing—the most successful entrepreneurs in history were paranoid—but you must be able to think about your fears rationally and be able to take educated risks.

When considering franchising, the overwhelming feedback, advice, and input you will receive will be biased against you starting a business. You must accept that even in the best of circumstances, you will be going against the grain of society to start your own business.

Getting comfortable with uncertainty is an acquired skill, and you can learn it like anything else—through practice. Those people close to you may not have this skill, so take in all the data points without being overly persuaded by any single person, except your spouse. Your spouse simply must be in alignment, or you will never move forward. Others from whom you can get input include:

- Family
- Friends
- Professional advisors

Take in advice from anyone whose opinion you value, but realize they will not have the perspective, research, due diligence or in-depth information you have about your brand. In the end, you will need to make an informed decision on your own.

12

WHAT TO EXPECT
AFTER SIGNING

People who are unable to motivate themselves
must be content with mediocrity, no matter how
impressive their other talents.

ANDREW CARNEGIE

One common question for new franchisees is: What happens
after I sign a franchise agreement? This is understandable
due to the nature of the franchise development process.

While you are investigating a franchise, you will be working
with a dedicated and bustling brand team whose only job is to
shepherd candidates through the investigation process. It's possible
your contact through the investigation process was a closely-
aligned third party sales firm hired by the franchisor to help them
handle the high volume of franchise candidates required to obtain
a small number of new franchisees. In either case, your company
contacts will change as you convert from being a candidate to

becoming a franchisee. This may create anxiety at first but will quickly be resolved due to the benefits of the franchise system.

Here are some actions you should expect the franchisor to initiate with you immediately upon franchise signing:

TRAINING

Training is a critical support service you should expect to receive from the franchisor at all appropriate levels. This includes training for the franchise owner, key managers, service providers, and support staff. Although you may be training the lower-level staff directly, the franchisor should provide all the tools and materials to help you complete that task. At a minimum, you should expect the franchisor to provide training for you as a franchisee and provide you with the tools and materials to train your staff.

- *Training Fees.* Though handled in different ways by different companies, it's common for franchisors to charge a training fee that's paid upfront in addition to the franchise fee. This will usually cover the critical initial training meetings both at company headquarters and at your franchise location. If not upfront, expect to potentially encounter required training charges and conference charges under your franchise agreement.

- *Franchisee.* The franchise owner training will vary in length but typically runs a week at the company headquarters to go over ownership roles, hiring of key employees, and launching your business in each function, such as real estate, operations, and marketing. Leaders of each functional support area for the franchisor will typically lead the training for you during the owner training. This is also a great chance to meet all of the support and executive team members for the franchisor, so take advantage of the opportunity, attend all events and spend time meeting the corporate team in addition to essential bonding with your fellow franchisees.

- *Key Managers.* Depending on the brand and model (owner-operator, executive, or semi-absentee), there is likely training for the primary day-to-day leader operating your business. This could be you or a manager you hire. In either case, the franchisor should provide extensive training for your key managers with ongoing resources, online portals, learning management systems, and opportunities for refresher training. Since you may need to hire new key managers in the future, there should be an ongoing program for onboarding and training new managers.

- *Staff.* This will typically involve training materials in the form of manuals, documents, and videos that you or your manager will use to train your staff. It wouldn't be cost-effective to pay for travel for your less-skilled hourly staff to attend training in person or for the franchisor to travel as you hire new personnel.

- *Grand Opening.* Depending on your business and industry, it is typical for the corporate team to send a trainer to your location to help you for a week or two during your actual grand opening. These trainers are often dedicated support personnel who travel and help open new sites in the respective system. Your franchisor should provide an individual who will help guide you through your actual launch. Afterward, they should be available to answer questions and make sure you have a smooth transition to daily operations.

- *Learning Management Systems.* As previously mentioned, all franchisors should provide you with operations and training manuals to support you in training yourself and your employees on brand operations. In more recent years, there is a trend toward Learning Management Systems (LMS). These online repositories can handle all the training resources for a system through a dedicated web portal, including videos, online courses, and built-in accountability and tracking. These systems allow you to monitor the participation in and completion of all training courses to help you manage your business, improve customer experience, and reduce liability.

REAL ESTATE

If you require real estate space for your business, the franchisor should have a well-developed process for assisting you through site selection, buildout, and grand opening. For most people, the only significant real estate transaction they have completed is purchasing a personal residence. A commercial lease can be daunting, and the process of building out a leased space may require as many as 20 different contractors or service providers to complete the project. *Don't panic.* This is a place where the franchisor should have you nearly entirely covered.

- **Site Selection.** First, the franchisor should provide you with software analysis, demographics, psychographics, and other site-selection tools and reports to help you identify the highest value location. You should also confirm any franchisor site preferences or reports with your real estate broker and local market conditions.

- **Broker.** Your franchisor may have a preferred provider (usually national) that can refer you to a quality local commercial real estate broker, sometimes for a fee. Alternatively, you may know someone locally who can refer you to quality providers whom you can interview personally before deciding. This may also help you avoid some fees. The choice of broker is often made by the franchisee, but it is possible there is a required vendor. This is something you can ask during your due diligence.

    - Always hire a specialist if possible. As an example, if you need high-visibility retail space, then hire an experienced retail tenant representative broker to assist you.

    - Look for credentials. Professionals with designations such as CCIM (commercial real estate professional organization) and SIOR (for office and industrial brokers) are committed to an extra degree of ethics, training, and professional standards that provide a differentiation point for real estate brokers.

    - Trust their knowledge. An excellent real estate broker's primary value is understanding the market. They should know all the comparable deals done in your submarket, market rents, tenant improvement allowances, and other market terms to help you negotiate a favorable lease.

- Trust your instincts. While the broker is a real estate expert, they are not an expert in your industry. Take into account your broker's input on real estate metrics that impact your business, like demographics, drive times, access, and visibility. However, even as a new franchisee, you will know more about your business. You're also the one signing the lease and making guarantees. Likewise, your franchisor is an expert in your brand industry, but not your local real estate market. I always suggest that if the franchisor's site analysis, your broker's recommendations, and your analysis and instincts all agree, you probably have a quality location option for your business.

- *Letter of Intent.* Once you locate an acceptable space, your franchisor and real estate broker will assist you in negotiating the important business and economic terms of the lease. The Letter of Intent ("LOI") is the primary format for exchanging terms in commercial contracts. Either your franchisor or broker will have a template of an LOI you will use as a basis if there are unique buildout and physical specifications needed for your space. Letters of Intent are just that: They are non-binding expressions of the business terms and make it much more efficient to negotiate the essential terms before getting an attorney involved.

- *Real Estate Attorney.* Unlike a franchise agreement, a commercial lease is entirely negotiable on every single point, and there are a vast number of nuances. You should hire a real estate attorney to assist you in commercial lease documentation. Once your broker has helped you negotiate and agree to business terms, the executed LOI can be provided to your attorney to prepare the lease. Most commonly, the landlord will prepare the lease form, as they will likely have a required standard form lease for their property, with certain modifications allowed. Your attorney will assist you in making sure all the LOI terms are captured in the lease document.

OPERATIONS

Operating the business day-to-day is where the rubber meets the road in franchising. As a signed franchisee, you now have access to and will be provided with the brand's detailed operations manual, process, procedures, online tools, software, and other proprietary systems. There should be a checklist or resource for nearly everything you need to know to launch your business.

- *Operations Manual.* This should be the heart of the franchise system for your brand. If you have signed with a new or younger brand, you should realize this is an evolving document and stay on top of changes and updates as the brand grows. This document should provide detailed and specific instructions on delivering the product or service within brand standards. More recently, these documents are trending toward Learning Management Systems ("LMS"), which are online portals with all learning, training, videos, and other resources managed online for the benefit of franchisees.

- *Hiring Support.* There has been a lot of litigation and news lately in the franchising world about whether hourly employees are employees of the franchisee or franchisor. Most franchisors will carefully structure their platform to make sure all employees of the franchisee are legally considered that way. However, the franchisor should still be able to supply resources to assist you in hiring key managers, staff, and service professionals for your business. These resources can include job descriptions, recruiting resources, and best practices to follow.

- *Vendors.* Vendor management can be a mixed blessing for franchisees. There may be required vendors from which you need to purchase items, such as your store furniture, fixtures, and inventory. Having these brand-specific supplies prearranged can make it much more efficient for the franchisee to avoid time-consuming purchasing research and decisions, as well as providing group buying power to reduce costs. It also will be necessary to ensure brand consistency. However, any supplies or materials not related to revenue, such as janitorial supplies, employee relations, storage, operating supplies, and other items may be at the discretion of the franchisee, allowing you to source the lowest cost resources for the business.

- *Back Office.* Depending on the brand and industry, the franchisor may go above and beyond to provide back-office support, accounting, human resources, and other functions. Or it may be left to the franchisee. Owner-operator service brands may tend to offer more services in this area.

- *Call Center.* One of the developing trends in service brands is for the franchisor to handle inbound lead generation and schedule appointments or provide customer service through a centralized call center. This makes complete sense for efficiency and consistency within a brand. For those brands that offer this, it's a differentiator for improved customer experience and reduces the number of employees needed for the franchisee. For consumer brands in a fixed location, there may be software at the local level to assist with customer service or possibly a call center to set appointments.

MARKETING

Marketing can also trigger mixed reactions from franchisees. Most franchise owners never feel they have enough marketing, yet this is a costly, time-consuming expense that is hard to measure. It can be frustrating to customize to your local market. However, your franchisor should have a robust and helpful marketing program. It can be challenging to create a standardized national marketing campaign at the local level, so expect to find tools and resources to help you run your marketing for your location.

- *Marketing Fund.* Nearly all franchise agreements will have a one or two percent revenue marketing fee required in addition to the regular royalty. By regulation, this fee must be separated, used as intended, and cannot go directly into the franchisor's pockets. Newer franchises with few locations aren't likely to turn on the marketing fund until they get enough units open to make it meaningful. This must have an application both nationally and in your local market, but the use can include a wide variety of marketing initiatives, including social media, television or radio advertising, print, public relations, and other channels. There may often be a marketing fund committee comprised of both franchisees and representatives of the franchisor to oversee the use of marketing funds. Note that this is entirely separate from a franchisee's paid marketing, which will be needed in addition to any national campaigns.

- *Social Media.* Many studies show that word of mouth is the most potent marketing tool. And in today's world, that means social media. Every franchise should have a robust social media program, including tools for each location to customize and bring credibility to the brand at the customer level. The resources can take many forms, but at a minimum, you should expect the franchisor to provide branded graphics and access to digital marketing assets on a shared platform to be customized for your location. In some cases, franchisors will not allow franchisees to control their social media and will make it more centralized. This is an area to investigate to make sure you understand what parts of social media marketing you control.

- *Digital Assets.* As mentioned above, you should have digital assets available to you on a shared online platform. These are used for many applications, including social media, printed posters for your location or events, email campaigns, and other marketing activities.Grass Roots. This is one of the most effective strategies for marketing your small business as a franchisee. However, it can be time-consuming and challenging to delegate or execute, depending on your personnel structure. Ask your franchisor or fellow franchisee about best practices, checklists, and strategies to get your new business noticed in your community.

- *Advertising.* Advertising is expensive, period. The most expensive forms of advertising will be print, outdoor (billboards), television, and radio. Most small businesses don't have the budget for these high ticket methods. And most of these methods are wide distribution, meaning it is costly and doesn't necessarily target your desired demographic or audience. There are good reasons for the rising dominance of digital advertising, whether pay-per-click or on social media sites such as Facebook and Instagram. On these platforms, you can specifically target only your audience. For instance, if your brand only counts women as your target client, then it would be inefficient to pay for ads targeting men. On digital platforms, you can choose who your audience will be and also test run campaigns to see which are most effective. Online advertising may be more likely to fit the budget and needs of a small business in the modern economy. As your brand grows, the franchisor may institute more national advertising paid for by the marketing fund.

- *Email Marketing.* If you have repeat or recurring customers of any kind, email marketing will be vital to you. Many studies also find that it is the most effective form of advertising. There are many best practices you should consider in how to communicate with your audience through email marketing, but you will likely find it is the most effective and lowest-cost form of marketing you can do. Your franchisor should have a platform set up and included in your software or technology fee to execute this in addition to providing content, graphics, and templates.

SUMMARY

Once you sign a franchise agreement, the emotional requirements relax and you can get down to business. But it can create a new sense of uncertainty about what comes next. With robust due diligence, you should know what to expect, and any good franchisor will have you covered step by step.

Among the things you will focus on right after signing a franchise agreement include:

- **Training.** This is where the franchise system shines, and you should expect robust training plans for every level of your organization.
- **Real Estate.** If your brand requires customer-facing real estate, this will be the first task on your list, and the franchisor will have a process for you. Many brands will not schedule operations training until you have signed a lease.
- **Operations.** The operations manual, in whatever form, is the heart of a franchise brand's system and is the secret sauce to running your business. You will learn much of it at training, and the rest should be covered with various support resources.

- *Marketing.* Any solid franchise brand should have a proven marketing plan for success. It may require a meaningful budget, especially upon your launch. And while there will be plenty of resources and best practices to follow, this is an area where you can also get creative.

After you have signed the franchise agreement, it is time to take a breath, then focus on following the system to get your franchise launched for success.

CONCLUSION:
VISUALIZING YOUR FUTURE

It is not in the stars to hold
our destiny but in ourselves.

WILLIAM SHAKESPEARE

Some have said that if you want to be an entrepreneur, franchising isn't for you. What they mean is that in franchising, you need to follow a system to be successful, so those people who want to blaze a path and create an entirely new product or service shouldn't buy a franchise. While I certainly agree that to be successful in franchising you need to follow a system, I disagree with the idea that you're not an entrepreneur if you start a franchise business.

Starting any business is an entrepreneurial act by my definition. Franchise or not, it requires an emotional mix of confidence, willingness to do whatever it takes, and a burning desire to succeed at being your own boss. You don't have to start a tech firm in Silicon Valley to be considered an entrepreneur.

When I was growing up with those big dreams of working in business, I may have had little actual knowledge of how to get there, but I did have drive and desire. Someday I knew I would make it. Later, when I was 46 and for the third time in my life out of a job due to other people's decisions, that desire was finally fully realized. I engaged a franchise consultant. I took the plunge, started a business, became a franchisee, and felt at every moment along the way that I was an entrepreneur.

Being an entrepreneur who starts a franchise means you agree with the concept of scale and using proven systems and processes to your benefit. Most Silicon Valley entrepreneurs will bring over systems and methods from previous companies or their investors, so they aren't creating the wheel from scratch. The only difference is their concept is usually novel and unproven.

Alternatively, in a franchise, your concept has been proven viable and successful at least in a handful of markets if not nationally, and the routine, back-office time-sucking tasks have been streamlined. This allows you to leverage your time most efficiently and work on, instead of in, your business. Minimizing time on redundant back office tasks is hugely powerful if you want to be able to start a business while maintaining a personal life.

Building a successful franchise business requires every attribute and definition of an entrepreneur, with fewer sacrifices. You can open a company with a built-in structure that allows you to maintain a personal balance in your life. Working 24 hours per day on a startup business that has a very low likelihood of success may be glamorized in the media, but the real statistics bear out that franchise ownership is vastly more successful. You should be proud of taking your first step on the road less traveled while smartly reducing your risk.

Most of the benefits of starting a franchise business and becoming an entrepreneur aren't financial, even though most candidates disproportionately focus on that factor. The intangible benefits of having professional and personal freedom, controlling your destiny, and achieving your positive future vision bring balance and satisfaction to your life that being an employee can never provide.

Think about your future, build your vision, and see where you want to go. Then decide if franchising can help you get there. If you can visualize your future, you can make it happen!

ABOUT THE AUTHOR

David Busker has navigated and succeeded in a zig-zagged yet upward entrepreneurial journey. With deep experience in multiple aspects of business as a CEO, CFO, CPA, business owner, startup founder, and multi-unit franchisee, he is in a unique position as a franchise consultant to advise future entrepreneurs.

As a franchise consultant, David has helped hundreds of candidates navigate the transition from employee to entrepreneur. His unique insights from both leading and starting businesses, as well as a no-nonsense educational approach, have endeared him to candidates seeking franchise ownership.

Being a franchisee, David fully understands the emotional demands and mental transition candidates need to go through to make the switch from working for others to owning their future. He helps candidates set their criteria, matches them to the perfect franchise, and guides them through the process of becoming a franchise owner.

David has enjoyed the empowering transition to business ownership and entrepreneurship and is passionate and dedicated to assisting others to do the same. David lives in Saint Louis, Missouri, with his wife and three daughters.

Learn more about David at ***www.franchisevision.com.***

Thank You for Reading

I hope you enjoyed reading this book
and found the content helpful in your
exploration of franchising. I appreciate all
forms of feedback and would be honored
if you would consider leaving
a review on Amazon.com at

https://www.amazon.com/dp/1733671706

to let me and others know what you
thought of the book.

Thank you so much!

START
YOUR JOURNEY
TODAY!

Learn more about franchising and if it's right for you by setting up a call with David Busker today. You can also sign up to get free resources, monthly insights on entrepreneurship and franchising, and stay abreast of the hottest franchise concepts.
To get started visit:

www.franchisevision.com

Made in the USA
Monee, IL
28 August 2021